UNFOLDING THE MYSTERY

Monastic Conferences on the Liturgical Year

Ecclesiae Matri
Fratribusque monasterii

UNFOLDING THE MYSTERY

Monastic Conferences on the Liturgical Year

Dom Hugh Gilbert, OSB

GRACEWING

First published in 2007

Gracewing
2 Southern Avenue
Leominster
Herefordshire HR6 0QF

ISBN 0 85244 093 6
978 0 85244 093 3

Typeset by Action Publishing Technology Ltd,
Gloucester GL1 5SR

Contents

Contents

19. 'Come, Holy Spirit!'   125
20. Mary Assumed into Heaven   128
21. With All the Saints   135
22. The Parousia: Sure and Certain Hope   138
23. Christian Joy   146

Note

Scriptural references are taken from the RSV Bible, unless specified otherwise.

Preface

I knew Pluscarden before it was reborn as a monastic community. I went there as a child with my parents and we would have a picnic in the cloister garden. Mr Grant kept things tidy from his home in the lodge, still occupied by his daughter Helen.

The very sun-drenched stones of the Priory – for that is what it was in pre-Reformation days – spoke of its past as a place of prayer and community life, and I remember my father expressing his hope that one day it would live again. He was not to see the re-opening day, but I was there as one of the Bishop's attendants, carrying the *bugia*, or candle stick. Since then the priory church has been re-roofed, the cloisters partially restored and much other necessary and beautifying work accomplished.

I was recently in the Holy Land. Our guide – a Syrian Orthodox Christian – kept reminding us that the Church was not in the stones he showed us, though they bore eloquent testimony to past faith, but in the community of faith which still lives in those lands. The same can be said of Pluscarden, now home again to a Benedictine community and raised to the dignity of an Abbey. The living stones are the monks. Together they form a house in which the Spirit dwells. If in this place, as the Abbey's motto proclaims, God gives peace, it is through their constant prayer, their glorious liturgy and their ennobling work.

The role of the Abbot is crucial to this spiritual building, and in these beautiful conferences and instructions which

Abbot Hugh has been persuaded to publish, we see the work of the master builder.

Since every grace is *ad ecclesiam* – for the upbuilding of the Church – I welcome, on behalf of all who read this book, the stimulus which this work will give to that personal enterprise of stone cutting which enables all of us to be fitted out as living stones in that building, which, aligned on Christ, provides sanctuary for the world's wayfarers, a place of peace and a well of inspiration – the Church.

May the Lord who inspires every good work bring this one to completion.

+Mario Conti
Archbishop of Glasgow
Glasgow, Candlemas 2007

Introduction

'It is with some hesitation,' says St Benedict in his *Rule*, 'that we determine the measure of others' food and drink', and it is with something of the same hesitation that these monastic conferences have been put together, edited for a more general audience, and offered to whoever may care to read them. It may alleviate perplexities to say that the monastic conference (this use of the word goes back to the fifth-century *Conferences* of the monk and abbot, St John Cassian) is a dish on its own, a distinct form of intended nourishment. It is not a doctrinal statement or a theological lecture, even if hopefully it includes some teaching of substance. Nor is it simply a homily or *ferverino*, even if hopefully it encourages those who hear it. Rather, it takes a subject or theme, usually from Scripture, the liturgy, monastic literature and life, and develops it in a free, somewhat informal way, always with an eye to the situation of the listening community, and always presupposing a Christian monastic culture. It is essentially a heart to heart (without bypassing the head) from a superior to his often long-suffering brethren. It is also, of course, a bottle thrown into the sea. Who knows where it will wash up, what help it may give? And who knows, in the present instance, to what extent it can speak to those outside the monastery?

At another level, though, any hesitancy may politely be shown the door. The following conferences, and the homilies added to them, turn on the feasts and seasons of the liturgical year, a natural enough subject in a Benedictine monastery where 'nothing is to be preferred to the work of God', or common prayer. As Gregorian chant has its eight modes, so the liturgy of a monastic community (occupying three to four hours a day in the author's experience) is always set to the 'mode' of a Sunday or weekday, of a season of the year, of a feast of the Lord or of his mother or of a saint, and this 'mode' permeates the whole life of the monastery. And here, monks like to think, the monastery may quietly claim to be a microcosm of the whole Church, a pattern for it. The Second Vatican Council formulated the status of the liturgy in unforgettable terms when it called it 'the summit and source of the Church's activity'. Liturgy, indeed, is not the whole of Christianity, but it – and even such a feature of it as its weekly and annual cycle – is to permeate and form and energize the whole of Christian life. This is part of the Christian structure of things. What gives liturgy, though, this status? What *is* Christian liturgy? What makes it so worth entering in to, incorporating into one's personal life, taking as the matrix of one's prayer? A saying of Christ's from his last exchange with his disciples may have light to shed. The context is the institution of the Eucharist on the one hand, the imminence of his death and resurrection on the other. Jesus is talking about the Paraclete, the Holy Spirit, who will enter human history in a new way thanks to his coming 'passage' to the Father, and he says: *'He will glorify me, for he will take what is mine and declare it to you'* (Jn 16:14).

'He will glorify me.' This gives the role of the Holy Spirit in the economy of salvation: to draw humanity to recognition of Jesus as the Son, as the complete disclosure of the Father, of divine reality.

'He will glorify me *for he will take what is mine.'* The Holy Spirit will 'take', says Jesus, what belongs to the Son, 'what is mine'. What is this? What is it that belongs above all to Christ? What is his 'glory'? How did his Sonship find expression? The answer is his paschal mystery, that is, his death, resurrection and ascension considered as the supreme revelation of God's love in human history and as the wellspring of our reconciliation with the Father. It is this – the mystery of Christ's 'Passover' – that the Holy Spirit 'will take', will take to himself, make a 'spiritual', transcendent reality (without it ceasing to be bodily), and thus 'declare', proclaim, communicate, make visible, audible and credible to those with eyes to see, ears to hear and hearts to believe.

He *'will declare'* it, says Christ, *'to you'*, that is, to the disciples. He will declare it first and foremost to the disciples to whom he was talking at the Last Supper, the Apostles. The Holy Spirit declares, entrusts to them, the first believers and the founders of the Church, the true meaning and content of Christ's reality, of his paschal mystery. They in turn, guided by the Holy Spirit and obeying Christ's own initiatives, will translate this inmost reality of Christ not only into preaching and teaching but also into the words and signs of liturgy.

The liturgy of the Church, her public worship centred on the Eucharist and sacraments, is thus a joint work of the Spirit and of the Apostles who, in Catholic thought, live on in their successors, the bishops of the Church. But more essentially still, this liturgy is the arena where the Holy Spirit continues to 'glorify' Christ: to 'declare' his paschal mystery, to keep us in mind of it, to lead us into it, to prepare us for its full realization in the new heaven and earth we await. Thanks to the Holy Spirit, the paschal mystery remains a present, operative reality in human history, a spring of living water, flowing out of the 'paradise' of the liturgy and watering the desert of the human heart and human life. It is this which gives our liturgies, so often humanly poor (what else could they be?), their divine value.

'In the course of the year,' says Vatican II again (*Sacrosanctum Concilium* 102), 'she – holy mother Church – unfolds the whole mystery of Christ from the incarnation and nativity to the ascension, to Pentecost and the expectation of the blessed hope of the coming of the Lord.'

It is this unfolding of the mystery of Christ that the following conferences and homilies hope to serve in some small way.

I am most grateful to Eileen Grant for all she has done to make this volume possible.

Dom Hugh Gilbert, Abbot of Pluscarden

'Holy mother Church is conscious that she must celebrate the saving work of her divine spouse by devoutly recalling it on certain days throughout the course of the year. Every week, on the day which she has called the Lord's day, she keeps the memory of the Lord's resurrection, which she also celebrates once in the year, together with his blessed passion, in the most solemn festival of Easter. Within the cycle of a year, moreover, she unfolds the whole mystery of Christ, from the Incarnation and birth until the ascension, the day of Pentecost and the expectation of blessed hope and of the coming of the Lord. Recalling thus the mysteries of redemption, the Church opens to the faithful the riches of her Lord's powers and merits, so that these are in some way made present for all time, and the faithful are enabled to lay hold upon them and become filled with saving grace.'

(*Sacrosanctum Concilium* 102)

Part I

1

Beginning to Pray

He began to pray.

At first he recited in full two or three familiar prayers – 'Let God arise!', 'Whoso dwelleth under the defence of the Most High' – but after that he prayed in a flow of thought that formed itself unconsciously and without spoken words, only occasionally leaning on the support of certain powerful, memorable phrases that stuck in his mind: 'Thy most radiant countenance, O Giver of Life!' . . . 'O Mother of God, Thou that lovest God and art full of grace . . .' Then, in wordless prayer, he would return to the vaporous clouds, the mists swirling across the layers of his consciousness, which groaned and shifted like ice breaking up on the rivers in spring.

To express truly and completely the anguish which was burdening him, neither set prayers nor even his own words sufficed; the only means was to kneel upon aching knees (although he was now oblivious of the pain) and to gaze before him intently in silent devotion. This was the way he could lay before God the totality of his life and his present suffering. God must surely know that he had not spent his life in the service for the sake of personal glory or to wield power; the medals he wore were not mere adornments and he was praying for the success of his troops not in order to save his own reputation, but to serve the might of Russia, for much of her future destiny might depend upon this opening battle of the campaign.

He prayed that the victims of war might not die in vain; that there might be a reward for the sacrifice made by those who, struck down unawares by lead and iron, might not even have time to cross themselves before dying. He prayed for clarity to be granted to his anguished mind, so that on that crucial, topmost peak of time he might take the right decision – and thus ensure that those who gave their lives did not do so for nothing.

As he knelt, the full weight of his body pressing to the floor through his knees, he stared at the folding icon placed at the level of his eyes. Whispering, he prayed and crossed himself – and each time he did so the weight of his right arm seemed to grow less, the burden of his body seemed to lighten, and light filled his mind: soundlessly and invisibly the heaviness and darkness fell away from him, vanished, evaporated: God had taken all the burden upon Himself, for in Him lay the power to give rest to all who were heavy-laden.[1]

The man praying here is Samsonov, a Russian General; the scene is the early days of the battle of Tannenberg; disaster is on the horizon for the Russians. As a passage, it must be one of the few in contemporary literature portraying a person in prayer – and convincingly. Isn't it strange how many descriptions are allotted the sexual act, how few the act of prayer? And yet the first belongs to the things that pass and the latter to the things that last.

'He began to pray.' What Solzhenitsyn describes is the journey into prayer. Samsonov moves from 'the vaporous clouds, the mists swirling across the layers of his consciousness', from 'the anguish which was burdening him', into 'union with the powers above', surrender of the will, and at least a temporary lightening of the load, even physically. It's a movement from anguish to the angels, from below to above, from the earthly to the heavenly.

'He began to pray'. I'd like to try and say something of that beginning especially as a daily beginning, that journey especially as a daily journey.

'The main business of any poet is to keep the roots and sources clear', wrote George Mackay Brown to fellow-Orcadian, Ernest Marwick.

He starts with language, since that's the material he works in – 'purify the dialect of the tribe' – restore images, use words sparingly and accurately. For if the language gets fouled, then all values go – people think wrong, or sloppily, then all proportion and value are lost, life becomes meaningless or a nightmare ...

I have tried to open a few of the old springs that have become choked and neglected, in the hope that one or two folk, here and there, might taste and think again.[2]

It was Henri Brémond who wrote a famous book, *Poetry and Prayer*. Many indeed are the parallels between the craft of the poet and the craft of the monk.

The 'main business' of any monk, we can say, is 'to keep the roots and sources clear', to purify the language not just between man and man but between man and God, to clarify the roots and sources of his heart, the roots and sources of prayer. 'We know it is not on account of wordiness that we are heard, but rather through purity of heart and tears of compunction, and therefore prayer ought to be brief and pure' (*Rule* 20.3–4). The 'business' of the monk is to *begin* to pray, to turn to prayer repeatedly, to start on the journey, to unclog the spring, cut the channel, dig the trench, clear the undergrowth, mark the path. Cassian is a careful cartographer here. 'First,' he says, 'anxiety about fleshly matters should be completely cut off. Then, not only the concern for but in fact even the memory of affairs and business should be refused all entry whatsoever; detraction, idle speech, talkativeness and buffoonery should also be done away with; the disturbance of anger, in particular, and of sadness should be entirely torn out; and the harmful shoot of fleshly lust and avarice should be uprooted.'[3] Not for himself alone, be it said, does the monk struggle to keep the sources clear, however much it be this opening up which prepares him for heaven. George Mackay Brown modestly hoped that 'one or two folk' might catch a restored clarity of language from him. In fact, he hoped for more than that, as is clear from other remarks. And the monk, in the confidence of the mystical Body, hopes that his modest, daily, never quite consummated attempt, nonetheless repercusses positively and far; that his prayer somehow keeps prayer itself alive and pure. And lack of prayer is the single great cause of the world's unhappiness.

It must be said loud and clear, this *is* the monk's main business: to turn back to prayer, to start on the journey, again and again. It is to turn over the paper soiled with his own mental and emotional scrawling and write something better on the other side. It's like turning a door handle and going in to someone else's room. 'Let him simply go in and pray', says St Benedict (52.4). It is to stay on his knees, at least metaphorically, in the stubborn hope that the mists will scatter and the clouds lift and God's clear light touch him. According to St Macarius (*Homily* 49.3),

> When the soul is not reborn from the Spirit above its thoughts remain entirely earthbound, its mind concentrated on earthly matters to the fullest extent of its powers. But when the soul is made worthy to receive the divine regeneration and fellowship of the Spirit, it gathers all its thoughts together and taking them with it goes to the Lord to enter that heavenly dwelling not made by hands, and all its thoughts become spiritual, pure and holy on entering the divine sphere.

That perhaps sounds a trifle ecstatic. As we know, it's something very rooted: what we do with our mind when we wake up and get up, when we enter church, when the mill-wheel mind spins out of control, when a conversation is ended and we return to ourselves, when we suddenly have nothing to do. 'He began to pray.' It's the 'main business' of the monk.

This journey, this itinerary: it is something more than a personal effort. The path through the woods is not one we have to cut for ourselves; it is already laid. 'We have a great high priest who has passed through the heavens, Jesus, the Son of God' (Heb 4.14). 'We have confidence to enter the sanctuary by the blood of Jesus, by the new and living way which he opened for us through the curtain, that is through his flesh, and since we have a great high priest over the house of God, let us draw near with a true heart in full assurance of faith, our hearts sprinkled clean from an evil conscience and our bodies washed with pure water' (Heb 10.19–22). We 'have come to Mount Zion and to the city of the living God, the heavenly Jerusalem, and to innumerable angels in festal gathering' (Heb 12.22). In the chosen word of the Letter to the Hebrews, we have, thanks to the death, resurrection and ascension of Christ, 'access' to God, to the Father, to the throne of grace. Jacob's ladder has been raised up, the altar has been built, the Cross lifted up. Every Eucharist is a living witness to the restored relationship, the possibility of access, the journey of prayer. Every Eucharist is the Church's *raptus* or *transitus* out of this world to the Father. Pardon the image, but think of the A9. Through the passes and over the mountains, it opens up the lowlands to the highlands. 'It narrows itself to be expanded,' says St Gregory the Great of the praying mind;[4] it narrows itself to be expanded, like the journey into the northern expanses. There are even cycle tracks now – for the little souls who can't afford a car! The monk, by his consecration to God and his daily conversion to the journey of prayer, is a living sign of the open road.

For Adam the journey was easy, unthinking, made without toil. C. S. Lewis attempts to recapture the pre-lapsarian knowledge of God in his *Voyage to Venus*, perhaps with a measure of success. St Thomas writes of Adam:

'God made man upright' (Eccles 7.30). The divinely established uprightness of man meant that what was lower was subjected to what was higher, and the higher were not impeded by the lower. And so the first man was not impeded by external things from a clear and firm contemplation of intelligible effects, but saw them in the radiation of the first Truth with a natural knowledge or one inspired by grace[5]

– meaning that he contemplated God and all things in God with ease, *unimpeded*, his feet unsnared, unstumbling. For the blessed, at the other end of the story, the journey is simple ecstasy: face-to-face vision, a seeing of God as he is, with a total and totally free surrender of the will following, highest bondage and highest freedom.

> And so my mind, bedazzled and amazed,
> Stood fixed in wonder, motionless, intent,
> And still my wonder kindled as I gazed.
>
> That light doth so transform a man's whole bent
> That never to another sight or thought
> Would he surrender, with his own consent;

> For everything the will has ever sought
> Is gathered there, and there is every quest
> Made perfect, which apart from it falls short.[6]

Our own journey, through Christ the Redeemer, is a return to the contemplative grace we lost in Adam and a going on in hope to what has not yet been revealed except as surpassing all expectation: 'what eye has not seen'. We are not as attuned as Adam was, nor are we yet irresistibly bedazzled. We have neither the facility of paradise nor the fixity of heaven. Even for the redeemed, 'a perishable body weighs down the soul, and this earthly tent burdens the thoughtful mind' (Wis 9.15); the passions lay their many ambushes. The clouds part and the city is seen, but the mist comes back, the vision flickers and is lost. St Gregory speaks of the 'slanted windows' through which God is glimpsed. It is a toilsome journey, certainly. And yet something holds us to it. It is the one thing worth doing.

I remember the Australian Cistercian, Michael Casey, saying, apropos Cassian's teaching on compunction, that monks are presumed to be in state of torpor: in the clouds and mist and ice of Samsonov's heart. The major road blocks – at least that's what they are *prima facie* – are so well-known as hardly to need naming: unacknowledged, unrepented sin, sleep, depression, anger, deep grievances, habitual irritation, and so on. There are the preoccupations of work, of responsibility for others, sheer business. One of Cassian's immortal vignettes, given precisely in Conference 9, *On Prayer*, is of the poor workaholic monk, 'restlessly constructing and repairing unnecessary things and exerting himself in mundane distractions'; at the urging of the unseen Ethiopian 'pounding a very hard rock with a sledgehammer', carrying on even though exhausted, long after – so to speak – the bell has rung for the end of work (9, 6, 1–2). On this journey, Cassian says, 'it is a matter of our also rejecting with unwavering strictness of mind those things which cater to our power and which have the appearance of a kind of goodness' (ibid., 4). Things we tend to reject as trifles which can weigh quite as much as the great things. We can be defeated by so little: what the cooks do to potatoes, what the monk beside us in choir does to the music. And yet it's not really there the problem is. It's that the place of encounter is precisely the place of refusal also, whether we call it heart or mind or whatever. 'He made her to live in his own dwelling-place', we sing on feasts of Our Lady. What does this mean? What is this dwelling-place? Is it God himself? Prayer? And then there is the contrary verse of Israel in the desert: 'and they murmured in their *own* tents, and failed to hear the voice of the Lord.' The two tabernacles: my own or the Lord's. That is the choice.

The real stumbling block is living in one's own mind. Many of us often are, perhaps, introverts by nature; some by nurture. Life outside the mind – the encounters with others and all that – is simply so painful, or was at some critical point of development, that the mind becomes the place of refuge. Or perhaps I am just enamoured of my own intuitions, my own concepts, my own judgements, confuse them with the divine and fail to see how they impede me. What else is there, one may say? How can I stop having ideas about holy things, and feel instead the burning finger of God? How can I touch and taste? How can I know, not know about? How do the stumbling blocks become stepping stones, the idols icons? Where is the path through affirmation and negation to transcendence? 'He made her live in his own dwelling-place.' The monk is someone who waits in patience for that act of God, to be taken up, out of his own miserable tent, into the Lord's. 'And thou – what needest with thy tribe's black tents/Who hast the red pavilion of my heart?'[7] 'On that day', as the prophets say, another psalm-verse will be verified: 'on that day all their thoughts will perish' (Ps 145.4) – perish and be transformed. 'For, if we may speak in this way, when the thoughts of the mind have been seized by this purity and have been refashioned from earthly dullness to the likeness of the spiritual and the angelic, whatever they take in, whatever they reflect upon, and whatever they do will be most pure and sincere prayer.'[8]

'He began to pray.' 'Let him simply go in and pray ...' What helps? Well, everything, just as everything can hinder.

But let me just mention: First, the word, especially of psalmody, of phrases from the Psalms, or familiar prayers; the word of the holy Name. It rescues us from our own word. It feeds us on something other than ourselves. 'He made her to live in his own dwelling-place'; it has that power. It wells up from within. The Holy Spirit presses a key and the phrase comes up on the screen. It can be such a redemptive thing.

Second, acceptance one of another; love of the brethren, if you like; that is, patient love. And thus what so often drives us away from prayer becomes the road into it. My brother is an occasion of prayer. Until he is, I don't know him.

Third, need. Many a writer will say, 'I *have* to write'. Graham Greene called it a disease he couldn't shake off. And so with the monk, more and more, under the pressure of experience of self and others and the Holy Spirit: he *has* to pray. It's a matter of life and death, and, as the heart expands, as much for others as for himself and as much for himself as for others. He *has* to cry 'mercy'. He *has* to call down the Holy Spirit. It is painful – as any burning need is. And all the pain of the world flows into it. And where there is need, then there is desire, and where there is desire, a way is always found. The test is always what I do when I have nothing else to do. If it's always a hobby or a project or a distraction, I need to change. 'He began to pray.'

Today, we keep Our Lady's birthday, and the day of Pluscarden's re-birth, fifty-six years ago. 'He made her to live in his own dwelling-place.' 'It was always the aim of the monks of Caldey to devote themselves to the contemplative life' (*Customary of Pluscarden Abbey*). May Mary keep us faithful to this aim, faithful beginners in prayer.

Notes

1. Aleksandr Solzhenitsyn, *August 1914* (Bodley Head, London, 1972), p. 330.
2. Rowena Murray and Brian Murray, *Interrogation of Silence* (John Murray, London, 2004), p. 84.
3. St John Cassian, *Conferences* 9, III, 1.
4. St Gregory the Great, *Homilies on Ezekiel* II, 2, 12.

5. St Thomas Aquinas, *Summa Theologiae* I, 94, 1.
6. Dante, *Il Paradiso*, XXXIII, ll.97–103.
7. Francis Thompson, 'Arab Love Song' from *Works*, Vol. 1 (Burns & Oates Ltd, London, 1913) p. 168.
8. St John Cassian, *Conference* 9, VI, 5.

2

Prayer in the Divine Economy

A Sketch

*My house shall be called a house of prayer for all
nations.*

(Is 56.7)

*'The first, chief and proper duty of monks is the contem-
plation of divine things and constant union with God in
prayer. They must apply themselves to this assiduously.'*
Constitutions of the Subiaco Congregation 77

'Fish swim, birds fly, human beings pray.' We are made in
God's image, and the image that we are – a living, knowing,
loving image – naturally tends towards its original. We all
know St Augustine: 'You have made us for yourself, O Lord,
and our hearts are restless until they rest in you.' We are made
for dialogue, we can say. And we instinctively recognize that
we are summoned by Something or Someone to a dialogue that
is in some ways always on offer. In our pre-conscious, there
is always this pressure from the Transcendent, the Absolute,
the Eternal. 'You beset me behind and before, and lay your
hand upon me ... Where shall I go from your spirit, or where
shall I flee from your face?' (Ps 138.5,7). Prayer is natural to
the human being. It's one gift of Africa, not to mention Asia,
to remind the rest of us of this.

St John Cassian uses the image of down and feather:

The soul may be reasonably compared to the finest down and lightest feather which, if spared the onset and penetration of dampness from without, have so mobile a nature that at the slightest breeze they automatically rise upward. But ... any drop of water, any dampening by moisture ... and the pressure of the liquid will drag them down ... So too with our soul. If sin and worldly preoccupation have not weighed it down, if dangerous passion has not sullied it, then, lifted up by the natural goodness of its purity, it will rise to the heights ... and leaving things below ... will travel upward to the heavenly and the invisible. Hence ... the Lord's command: 'See to it that your hearts are not weighed down by drunkenness and intoxication, and the concerns of everyday life' (Lk 21.34).[1]

Yes, the human being is a praying animal. Traditional cultures are praying cultures. Our own culture is one which restricts the public expression of religion to definite times and places. This is unnatural. When we pray we are returning to, living in harmony with, our natural condition – doing what humans do. We are becoming what God intended from the beginning, a house of prayer. Christian faith holds that, from the very beginning of human history, man was destined to share in the life proper to God Himself. After the Incarnation we can say that this life is life in Christ, a share in that of the eternal Son given us by the Holy Spirit. And how can a filial life be anything other than a life of prayer?

The following is a somewhat amateur – though I hope in the good sense as well as the less so! – attempt to suggest just how central to the human and Christian enterprise prayer is, or again, how God's work in human history can be read as that of building, in us and of us, a house of prayer.

Prayer in the Beginning

According to St Paul (Rom 5.14) Adam 'was a type of the one who was to come', and therefore too of us/of man in Christ. In the Fathers of the Church and the great medieval theologians, we find a theology of original justice and the Fall centred on prayer. Adam, who was by nature a prayer, according to the image, was also a contemplative by grace, according to the likeness. Like Bunyan's pilgrim, his mind was stayed on God; he 'knew' God; he communed with God and the angels. From this infused focus upon God, there flowed his personal and social equilibrium, and his harmony with nature. All things prayed with him and through him.

'By means of grace Adam became like an angel in his knowledge of contemplation.'[2]

> Man was made right by God in this sense, that in him the lower powers were subjected to the higher, and the higher nature was made so as not to be impeded by the lower. Hence the first man was not impeded by exterior things from a clear and steady contemplation . . .[3]

The Fall, in consequence, was essentially, centrally, a turning of the mind and will from the grace-inspired, Spirit-inspired contemplation and knowledge of God. The house has become a house of something else. From that all the chaos and confusion followed, and ultimately, most tellingly, the collapse of death. 'You have changed the object of your contemplation,' say wise Carmelites to a sister confused by secondary things.

> Human beings, contemptuous of the better things and shrinking from their apprehension, sought rather what was closer to themselves . . . the body and its sensations. So they turned their minds away from intelligible reality and began to consider themselves . . . when . . . he [Adam] abandoned his thinking of God and began to consider himself, then they [Adam and Eve] fell into fleshly desires and realized that they were naked . . . They realized that they were not so much stripped of clothing as stripped of the contemplation of divine things, and that they had turned their minds in the opposite direction. For abandoning the consideration of a desire for the one true being, I mean God, from then on they gave themselves up to various and separate desires of the body . . .[4]

The Fall represented a movement away from contemplation and love of God to contemplation and love of self; from preoccupation with the supra-sensible to immersion in the sensible; from a unity derived from God contemplated to a dispersion in multiplicity.

The significance of this theology – which sees prayer as essential, in two opposing ways, to man's elevation and fall – is that it shows, in a reverse image, what the process of redemption will involve. It shows it as transition from the collapse of prayer – one could say the misdirection of prayer (the love of 'spectacle', of the flickering image; idolatry) – to its restoration and reconstruction. 'Even though he disobeyed you, you did not abandon him to the power of death, but helped all men to seek and find you. Again and again you offered a covenant to man, and through the prophets taught him to hope for salvation' (Eucharistic Prayer IV). 'When Adam fell, God's Son fell; because of the true union made in heaven, God's Son could not leave Adam, for by Adam, I understand all men.'[5]

Prayer in the Time of Promise and Preparation

'In the Old Testament, the revelation of prayer comes between the Fall and the restoration of man, that is, between God's sorrowful call to His first children: "Where are you? What is this you have done?" and the response of God's only Son on coming into the world: "Lo, I have come to do your will, O God"' (*Catechism* 2568).

Here again we see the centrality of prayer. We see it, first, in the Old Testament pictures of the righteous pagan: Abel and his offering; Enosh, son of Seth (the replacement of Abel), after whose birth Genesis says: 'At that time men began to call upon the name of the Lord'; Enoch who 'walked with God'; Noah who did likewise and who on emerging from the ark, humanity and the world beginning again, 'offered burnt offerings on the altar'; Melchizedech who brought out 'bread and wine' and was 'priest of God Most High'; Job, who after each of his sons' feats, 'would rise early in the morning and offer burnt offerings according to the number of them all ... Thus Job did continually'; think of Cornelius too, 'a devout man who feared God with all his household, gave alms liberally to the people, and prayed constantly to God' (Gen 4.4, 26; 5.22; 6.9; 8.20; 14.18; Job 1.5; Acts 10.2). Again and again the righteous pagan is a praying person.

A fortiori, the righteous Israelite: Abraham and the prayer of faith, Moses and the prayer of the mediator, David and the prayer of the king, Elijah, the prophets and conversion of heart. There are, to my mind, two great symbols in the Old Testament of the centrality of prayer, one monumental, one literary: the Temple and the Psalms.

When we read the book of Exodus, we can be tempted to divide it into the exciting and the boring. The exciting: the oppression in Egypt, the burning bush, the conflict with Pharaoh, the plagues, the crossing of the Red Sea, the theophany on Mount Sinai, the giving of the Law through Moses, the apostasy of the golden calf. The boring: the last six chapters about the building of the tabernacle. But this last is the goal of all that goes before. The climax of the book comes in chapter 40.34: 'Then the cloud covered the tent of meeting and the glory of the Lord filled the tabernacle.' The climax is the presence of the Lord in and over the tent, the glory filling the tabernacle. This is the 'trailer' as it were for the indwelling of the Temple in Jerusalem. The whole exodus leads to it. The purpose of the exodus is the building of this house, the house of prayer.

The climax of the whole 'Deuteronomic History' in turn – from Joshua to *2 Kings* – lies in Solomon's building and dedication of the Temple. The end is the Temple's destruction at the hand of ravaging pagans, the outward sign of Israel's fall from prayer. In 1 and 2 Chronicles, with Ezra and Nehemiah (which take us through to the rebuilding of the Temple in the Persian period), the centrality of the Temple is even clearer. The Book of Ezekiel, too, climaxes in the eight chapters (40–47) which describe the ideal reconstructed Temple. Then think of the place occupied in Jewish memory by the two great destructions of the Temple by the Babylonians and the Romans. The Temple was thought of as, literally, the centre of the world – built on the site of Abraham's sacrifice – the place to which the Gentiles would one day come. It was also thought of as the Garden of Eden, paradise regained.

The second great symbol of the place of prayer in the Old Testament is, of course, the Book of Psalms. The Psalms 'represent the corporate and personal worship of Israel in its purest form.'[6] They take us into the heart of Israel. They are one of the great moments – always valid (Christians use them too) – in the rebuilding of mankind as God's house of prayer.

Prayer in the Fullness of Time

'In the fullness of time, God sent His Son, born of a woman, born under the Law ...' The fullness of time brings us the fullness of prayer. The prayer that was initiated in the beginning, the prayer that God continued to incite in fallen humanity, the prayer that was being taught to Israel through all its purifying experiences, is now given, in a new fashion, in Christ. Christ is the new or second Adam: humanity restored to image and likeness. Christ is the new Temple: '"Destroy this temple and in three days I will raise it up." But he spoke of the temple of his body' (Jn 2.20–21). Christ is the Son of David, the true psalmist.

Above all, though, he is the Son of the Father. As such, he is – in his Person, in his 'constitution' so to speak – prayer personified or prayer consummated. His human nature was and is hypostatically united to his divine Person, and that Person is filial, is the Son of the Father. Therefore Jesus, from his human side, is united to the divine and turned to the Father in a quite unique way. In him, in his make-up, the union with God which Adam had lost is super-abundantly restored.

In terms of Our Lord's life, we must surely say that his constant dialogue with the Father is what was central. The Gospel of Luke particularly reveals it. The first words he speaks, as a twelve-year-old, are: 'Why were you searching for me? Did you not know that I must be in my Father's house [or, about my Father's business]?' (Lk 2.49) And his last words – on the Cross – are: 'Father, into your hands I commend my spirit' (Lk 23:46). On the place of prayer in the life of Jesus and, consequently, in the Christology of the Church, there's a suggestive essay by Joseph Ratzinger, in which he sums up his views in theses, of which the first three are:

1. According to the testimony of Holy Scripture, the centre of the life and person of Jesus is his constant communication with the Father.
2. Jesus died praying. At the Last Supper he had anticipated his death by giving of himself, thus transforming his death from within into an act of love, into a glorification of God.
3. 'Since the centre of the person of Jesus is prayer, it is essential to participate in his prayer if we are to know and understand him.'[7]

When we come, then, to the act of redemption itself, we can again think in terms of prayer. 'Instead of resorting to the analogy of human justice that is so different from God's, why doesn't the theology of redemption let itself be guided by the analogy of prayer?' asks F. X. Durrwell in *Christ our Passover*. 'Jesus,' he says, 'became redemption by becoming prayer ... The mystery of salvation is that a person (Jesus) became prayer for the whole world, and it was heard.' And, in a footnote he adds, 'The Christian would also learn with joy that his or her death, too, will be a final and better prayer.'[8]

'The prayer of Jesus accomplished the victory of salvation,' says the *Catechism* (2606). In obedience to the Father, the Son gives himself in prayer and sacrifice for us sinners who have turned away from prayer. On the Cross, the Son continues in prayer. Despite the ruining onslaughts of the powers of the evil, he remains in God's house. The prayers the Gospels record are only the visible flames of the invisible, filial fire. 'My God, my God, why have you forsaken me' (Mt 27.46); 'Father, forgive them; for they know not what they do' (Lk 23.34); 'Father, into your hands I commit my spirit' (Lk 23.46); 'I thirst' (Jn 19.28). When the soldier pierces his side with the lance, it is this Temple which is opened. And when, in the Resurrection, the Father hears the Son, hears this prayer, and raises him to eternal life, he makes him the house of prayer for all nations.

Prayer in the Time of the Church

By the gift of the Spirit that follows, the Church is brought into being and brought into being precisely as a share in the sonship of the Son, and in his filial prayer. 'Our Father...' She enters the house, she is the house. The community of faith cannot be other than a community of prayer. It's striking that the first picture of the post-Ascension community, given in Acts 1:12ff, is of the eleven 'with one accord devoting themselves to prayer, together with the women and Mary the mother of Jesus, and with his brethren'. This perspective is maintained throughout Acts. The day of Pentecost, for example, begins in prayer: 'They were all together in one place' (this 'one place' is the place of prayer) and ends in the same: three thousand were baptized that day, and 'they devoted themselves to the Apostles' teaching and fellowship, to the breaking of bread and the prayers' (Acts 2.1,42).

We are surely meant to believe that it is Stephen's Christ-like prayer at his stoning, 'Lord, do not hold this sin against them', that is answered by Saul's conversion. Peter's deliverance from prison has 'earnest prayer' behind it, 'made to God by the church'. Paul's first missionary journey is mandated by the Holy Spirit while the church at Antioch is 'worshipping the Lord and fasting' (Acts 7.60; 12.5; 13.2). And so on, not only in Acts but throughout the New Testament. It is clear that the New Testament Church is a praying Church, a house of prayer.

And so, by the power of the Spirit, the Church remains. Thinking of corporate prayer, we say with Vatican II that 'the liturgy is the summit toward which the activity of the Church is directed; it is also the source from which all her power flows'.[9] And the place that liturgy holds in the Body as a whole, prayer – liturgical and private – surely holds in the life and soul of each living member.

The Church's centre and the centre of the life of every Christian individual is the Eucharist and the high point of the Eucharistic celebration is called, tellingly, the Eucharistic Prayer. The Church is a praying Church – giving thanks, offering, interceding.

[I'd like to emphasize the place of intercession. 'First of all, then, I urge that supplications, prayers, intercessions, and thanksgivings be made for all men' (1 Tim 2.1). The figure of the intercessor emerges in the Old Testament: Abraham, Moses, Elijah, Jeremiah, the Suffering Servant. Israel as a whole has the mission of interceding for the Gentiles. Christ is the Intercessor, par excellence, but in the Spirit the Church shares in this. 'If Christians are to live together, they will pray together, and united prayer is necessarily of an intercessory character, as being offered for each other and for the whole, and for self as one of the whole ... Intercession [is] a token of the existence of a Church [which is] Catholic.'[10] The early Christians had such a vivid sense of this that they coined the proposition: 'the world is kept in being by the prayer of Christ.' The theology here is that, since Christ, human history continues simply so that the number of the elect may be completed, that people may be gathered into the Church, that the house of prayer for all peoples be brought to its fullness. And the Church, through her intercession, first of all, shares with God in this work of extending the redemption.

The figure of Mary should not be passed over here. She is a type of the Church, and her role in heaven is seen above all as that of intercession. 'Her office above,' as Newman says, 'is one of perpetual intercession for the faithful Militant ... and, in the eternal enmity which exists between the woman and the serpent, while the serpent's strength is that of being the Tempter, the weapon of the Second Eve and Mother of God is prayer.'[11] In the catacombs, there are the famous representations of the woman with uplifted hands – *orans* (praying). She is both the Church and Mary at their essential task of intercession.]

Prayer cannot be less 'the life' (as Newman calls it) of the individual Christian than it is of the Church. The Christian is a redeemed son or daughter of God, and cannot but express his or her faith, hope and love in the form of prayer – adoring, blessing, thanking, praising, interceding. It is in and through prayer that the effects of the Fall are reversed and the personality rebuilt. Central here is what the New Testament calls 'unceasing prayer', persevering prayer. It is found in the earliest document of the New Testament, 1 Thessalonians 5.17: 'pray constantly' or 'unceasingly'. 'Be constant in prayer' (Rom 12.12; Eph 6.18; 1 Cor 1.4; 1 Tim 2.8). 'Pray at all times in the spirit, with all prayer and supplication.' 'I give thanks to God always for you,' says St Paul to the Corinthians. 'I desire then that in every place the men should pray, lifting holy hands without anger or quarrelling.' These phrases are the origin of the 'always and everywhere' of our Prefaces. It is not a deep enough interpretation to call this mere hortative hyperbole. The Christian is a praying animal, and prayer will tend to impregnate the whole of his or her life – from the heart upwards and outwards. 'And he told them a parable, to the effect that they ought always to pray and not lose heart' (Lk 18.1).

Prayer and the End

'The Spirit and the Bride say, "Come". And let him who hears say, "Come" . . . Come, Lord Jesus!' (Rev 22.17, 20). 'What sort of persons ought you to be in lives of holiness and godliness, waiting for and hastening the coming of the day of the Lord' (2 Pet 3.11–12). 'Let grace come and this world pass away' (*The Didache*).

Prayer anticipates the End. According to St Thomas Aquinas, 'Prayer is a means which partakes of the nature of the end.' When we pray, we anticipate the vision and possession of God proper to the life of glory. When we pray, we already stand in the light of God's face and anticipate the judgement. More than that, we *hasten* the End. 'Come, Lord Jesus', prays the Bride full of the Spirit, 'hastening' the return of the Lord, the consummation of history, the completion of the house; hastening all this by her prayer and patience. So too in every Lord's Prayer. So too in every Eucharist. Every Eucharist hastens the End. And that End will be the consummation of prayer in vision and possession, in a new creation.

And I saw no temple in the city, for its temple is the Lord God the Almighty and the Lamb. And the city has no need of sun or moon to shine upon it, for the glory of God is its light, and its lamp is the Lamb. By its light shall the nations walk; and the kings of the earth shall bring their glory into it, and its gates shall never be shut by day – and there shall be no night there; they shall bring into it the glory and the honour of the nations.

(Rev 21.22–26)

Notes

1. St John Cassian, Conference IX, 4.
2. Aquinas, *De Ver.* Q. 18, a. 2, ad. 4.
3. Ibid., *Summa Theologiae*, 1a, 94, 1.
4. St Athanasius, *Contra Gentes* 3.
5. Julian LT 51.
6. Evelyn Underhill, *Worship* (Nisbet, London, 1937, 2nd edn), p. 214.
7. Joseph Ratzinger, *Behold the Pierced One* (Ignatius, San Francisco, 1987), pp. 15, 22, 25. Cf. E. Underhill, *Worship*, pp. 220–221.
8. F. X. Durrwell, *Christ our Passover* (Redemptorist Publications, 2004), pp. 54, 180.
9. Second Vatican Council, *Sacrosanctum Concilium* 10.
10. John Henry Newman, *Parochial and Plain Sermons* III, pp. 352–3.
11. Ibid., Letter to Pusey, p. 73.

3

Standing at the Altar

He lay in a crib so that you could stand at the altar.[1]

The Mass always has more to give us. It tells us everything about God and also everything about ourselves, and we will never get to the end of it. 'He lay in the crib so that you could stand at the altar': one of those pithy and paradoxical sentences that the Fathers coined so easily. One of the almost infinite possible expressions of the 'wonderful exchange', first formulated by St Paul: 'Though he was rich, yet for your sake he became poor, so that by his poverty you might become rich' (2 Cor 8.9), and formulated most classically as the Son of God becoming the Son of Man so that the sons of men might become the sons of God. One of those patristic dicta, therefore, that take us into the heart of the Christian faith. God affirming us, by denying Himself; God humbling Himself to lift us up; God giving Himself by emptying Himself, asking emptiness of us only to flood us. What is intriguing about this particular formulation (owed to St Ambrose) is the image chosen for the term of the process: standing at the altar. He lay, a helpless baby, not yet capable of toddling, so that we could stand; we who were made upright but have fallen. He lay in the crib, a manger, an animal's eating trough, so that we could stand at the altar, the place where man meets God and feeds on Him.

In the anamnesis of Eucharistic Prayer II, the Church prays: 'In memory of his death and resurrection, we offer you, Father, this life-giving bread, this saving cup. We thank you for counting us worthy to stand in your presence and serve you.' Here we meet the same idea: standing at the altar, standing in your presence. I presume that neither the Church in this prayer, nor St Ambrose, mean to restrict this being at the altar to the clergy. The whole Christian people is in view. And for both, standing before the altar, standing in the presence of the Father is a symbolic shorthand for being redeemed, for being Christian.

We need to think, as the Church and the Fathers do, neither simply literally nor simply symbolically, but 'real-symbolically' as the Germans say. Jesus did actually lie in a crib, but this lying in the crib was an expression of something more than a material fact. He lay in the crib because he humbled himself to become a human being in all the stages of human life. And what was expressed by lying in the crib was also expressed by being conceived and carried in a womb, by being born, by growing up, by suffering the onslaught of the Evil One, by feeling tired and hungry and above all by the events of the Passion. He humbled himself even to death, death on a cross. And so with the counter-side of all this: our standing at the altar. St Ambrose means that literally. One could think of the Eastertide hymn *Ad cenam Agni* (*At the Lamb's high feast*): redemption is there expressed in the gathering of all at the Eucharist. Yet obviously this being at the altar is only ever a temporary thing: half an hour a day or one hour once a week. So it is symbolic as well as literal. The Christian is always standing at the altar. When he does so literally and transitorily, he is only expressing – and, one hopes, renewing – what he is doing really, inwardly, always. Standing at the altar is only one expression of the end product of redemption, just as lying in the crib was only one expression of the bringing about of redemption. But it is powerful enough and worth thinking about. 'Lying in the crib' says Incarnation; 'standing at the altar' says Eucharist. The mysteries answer each other, and deep is calling on deep.

The Eucharist teaches us about ourselves and the Eucharist means standing at the altar. It is *the* place for Christians to be: their redemption *and* their vocation. Standing at the altar, therefore, means standing by the Cross, standing before the

Father, standing in the Spirit; these cannot really be separated. If we stand at the altar, it is because we have been baptized. And if we have been baptized we have been attached to the Cross. Attachment to the Cross means at once a breaking with sin and a widening of the heart. Walter Hilton wrote about the battle with the dark image; we take that battle into the Mass and everywhere. For an icon to be worthy of the liturgy, the icon writer must first purify his or her heart; even each ingredient of an icon must die and rise. If we want to get somewhere, we must leave somewhere. Then the heart opens.

That universality, that extension of the arms, that embrace is asked of us by standing at the altar. It is indeed I who stand. 'He lay in the crib so that you (*tu*) might stand at the altar.' But who am 'I'? 'Christian prayer to the Father is not the call of a soul that knows nothing outside God and itself, but is bound to the community of our brothers, together with whom we make up the one Christ, in whom and through whom alone we are able to say "Father", because only through Christ and in Christ are we His "children".' Can a hermit priest celebrating alone legitimately say, *Dominus vobiscum* ('the Lord be with you' in the plural)? Yes, says St Peter Damian, because each member carries the whole body in himself, because each believer in some real sense represents the whole Church. Because, in the Christian view, the individual human being is a person, that is, 'not a replaceable part of the whole, but a unique and unrepeatable being in whom the whole (all humanity and indeed all creation) is mysteriously present' (A. M. Allchin). Because 'in the measure in which he is a person in the true theological sense of the word, a human being is not limited by his individual nature. He is not only a part of the whole, but potentially includes the whole, having in himself the whole earthly cosmos, of which he is the hypostasis' (Vladimir Lossky).

Standing at the altar is standing in the place human beings are meant to stand in. It is the most human place to be. It is home. Standing at the altar means crucifying all that is selfish in oneself by the fear of the Lord and opening the heart to everyone and everything; or, as Cardinal Hume put it, saying no to oneself and yes to others. It means turning with such a heart – a pure heart, an expanded heart – to the Father. In his Apostolic Letter *Orientale Lumen*, John Paul II said this of the monastery (and monastery and altar are one and the same):

> The monastery is the prophetic place where creation becomes praise of God and the precept of concretely lived charity becomes the ideal of human co-existence; it is where the human being seeks God without limitation or impediment, becoming a reference point for all people, bearing them in his heart and helping them to seek God (9).

This is the point about prayer made most succinctly by Henri de Lubac: 'prayer is essentially the prayer of all for all.' Naturally, we pray for friends and family; but however particular 'prayer is essentially the prayer of all for all'. That is what Vladimir Lossky and St Peter Damian are saying. That is standing at the altar.

When, perhaps in AD 156, the police came to arrest the eighty-six-year-old Bishop of Smyrna, Polycarp,

> he only requested that they might grant him an hour to pray undisturbed. When they consented, he stood up and began to pray facing the east, and so full was he of God's grace that he was unable to stop for two hours, to the amazement of those who heard him, and many were sorry that they had come out to arrest such a godlike old man. Finally he finished his prayer, after calling to mind all those who had ever come into contact with him, both important and insignificant, famous and obscure, and the entire Catholic Church scattered throughout the world. It was now time to go, and so they put him on a donkey ... (Acts 7,8)

In 259, a Spanish bishop on his way to martyrdom, Fructuosus, said to all in a loud voice: 'I must bear in mind the entire Catholic Church spread abroad in the world from East to West' (*Passion* 3).

An icon of St Silouan, the twentieth-century monk of Mt Athos, shows him holding a scroll with the text of a prayer that was his: 'I pray thee, O merciful Lord, for all the peoples of the earth, that they may come to know thee by thy Holy Spirit.'

Such is 'standing at the altar.' Such is the prayer that both the Lord's Prayer, and the Church's Prayer par excellence, the Eucharistic Prayer, teach us. It's the prayer of the Cross, 'calling together all the dispersed, from all the corners of the earth, to the knowledge of the Father'.

St Benedict sees the way of the monk as a returning to God. And it has come home to me recently that what we are doing in the liturgy, what we are empowered to do, is not just return by our single selves, but return the whole world, and all humanity, and one another to God. Everything comes from Him, from the Father, through Christ in the Spirit, and in the Spirit, through Christ, everything returns to the Father. This is the work of God and we are co-opted into it. It's the work of leading the world into God's joy. Of itself this is completely beyond us. It is a supernatural work, and we unworthy workmen with a seemingly limitless capacity for spoiling His purposes. We are afraid of the way of surrender, afraid of the way of love. We are full of misgivings. But 'he lay in the crib' and we have been brought to the altar. And there in the Spirit we stand and *dare* to call God Father, sharing 'the prayer of all for all'.

Note

1. St Ambrose, *Exposition of the Gospel of St. Luke*, II, 41. Latin: *ille in praesaepibus, ut tu in altaribus*. The English translation used here takes the liberty of expanding St Ambrose's concision by the rendering, 'he *lay* in the crib, so that you *might stand* at the altar.'

Part II

4

The Coming of Christ

We are about to embark on a new liturgical year, and on Advent. Some thoughts on these. I remember once travelling north on the East Coast route and being struck by the succession of Yorkshire villages we swept through. It was almost like a glimpse of pre-industrial Britain, at least if you didn't look too closely. There was each village, *sibi compacta in idipsum* ('bound firmly together') like the Jerusalem of the Psalms, a whole, an integrity, a little self-sufficient concentration of human life. Here was geographical space humanized. And in every village was a church, and in every case the church was the building that first caught the eye, that stood out, tall, shapely, the centre (even when it wasn't), the symbol of transcendence. We talk of the liturgical year and the Divine Office as the sanctification of time. Here was physical and human space sanctified, Christianized.

The train sped on to Scotland. Another space. Were one a postman, one might cry out, 'Ah, the land of fifteen postal areas!' Were one a civil servant, 'Hail to the land of thirty-two councils!' Thinking as a Christian, one might again observe the churches, signs of the Christian sanctification of this space. And as a Catholic one might even think, here is the land of two ecclesiastical provinces and eight dioceses. Here I am, as the train goes further north, about to enter the territory of our bishop. Because not only physical churches but ecclesiastical jurisdictions represent a sanctification of space.

And what do we mean by this phrase, sanctification of space? We mean that thanks to the presence of a bishop (and therefore of priests), and thanks to churches, God's holy word and sacraments are present and available in this physical and human space. We mean therefore that those within this space can now be sanctified, and that through them this physical and human space can become, in some sense, God's holy Temple.

Changing what has to be changed, we must mean something similar when we talk of the sanctification of time, even if the latter is a concept less easy to grasp. Time and space are the two dimensions in which we live our lives. When we talk of the sanctification of time, we mean that there are holy things present in our chronological and human time (or times). We mean that, within time, there are special times set apart for God, just as within space, there are special places set apart for God. We mean that time is ordered not only by physical and human criteria (years, seasons, months, weeks, days, hours, minutes etc.) but also by ecclesial criteria (Advent-Christmas, Lent-Easter, Morning Prayer and Evening Prayer etc.), just as physical and human space is also measured by provinces and dioceses and other forms of ecclesiastical territory. We mean therefore that those who live in this time can be sanctified, and all they do and all that happens to them. We mean that Christ, to whom 'all time belongs' is present in this time too.

The liturgical year and the Divine Office are a presence of Christ. And the presence of Christ is transforming. What would our year be like without the liturgical year? What would our day be like without the Office? The circuit of the earth around the sun – the solar year – is hallowed by the liturgical year. The earth's turning on its own axis – the day – is filled by the daily celebration, however many times a day, of psalms and hymns, readings and prayers, not to mention the Mass. 'Christ yesterday and today, the beginning and the end, Alpha and Omega, all time belongs to him, and all the ages, to him be glory and power through every age for ever.' So says the celebrant at Easter, proclaiming Christ as the Lord of time, every year and every day belonging to him and coming into being so as to be taken into the 'fullness of time'. Once one has experienced something of this, how empty life feels without this Christianization. The liturgical year, like the daily round of the Office, is a work and a task, it's a road for travelling down as long as we're in time, it's a commitment and a loyalty, but first of all it's a gift, it's a presence, it's something to be grateful for. It's a filling of our emptiness. I just spotted this, this morning, in a book on Augustan Culture: '*Praesens,* the equivalent of the Greek *epiphanes* ... means both "physically present", "alive", and "lending assistance", "propitious", "powerful".' That's the Christ of the liturgy.

II

We are about to embark on Advent. Perhaps St Benedict's saying, 'Whatever good work you begin, ask him with most earnest prayer to perfect it' has a place here. We can ask the Lord for help in celebrating these five weeks. May I offer three thoughts.

The first concerns a word. It is possible to take the Epiphany as the climax of Advent and Christmas, and in the same way it's possible to take the word 'Advent' – which is another translation of Epiphany – as describing not just the weeks before Christmas but the time after it as well: the whole Advent-Christmas-Epiphany cycle. The Introit for the Epiphany opens with the words: *Ecce advenit* ... 'Behold, he comes!' It's good to look at it as a whole.

It may help to remember that the liturgy took shape in the period historians call Late Antiquity, let's say from the fourth to the seventh century. Just as the Bible is marked, through and through, by the culture of the ancient Near East, so the liturgy is permeated by the culture of the later Greco-Roman world, And in that world the word 'Advent' was a far more resonant one then than now. It belonged to the ancient world's understanding and cult of the ruler. It denoted the Coming of a King, an Emperor to a city, 'Behold, your King comes to you', says Scripture, and the entry of Christ into Jerusalem bears some of the marks of such an Advent. This is why it was for long a Gospel read on the First Advent Sunday. This 'metaphor', the Ruler's state arrival in a city, fills the Advent

and Christmas liturgy. The texts of the prophets about the
Messiah or the kingship of Yahweh are amalgamated with the
'Advent' Ceremonial of the Greco-Roman world, just as are
the descriptions of the Parousia in the Pauline letters.

Here's an example of an *Adventus*. In the summer of 585
the Merovingian King Guntram 'visited' Orleans. As Gregory
of Tours tells us:

> A vast crowd of citizens came out to meet him, carrying flags and
> banners, and singing songs in his praise. The speech of the
> Syrians contrasted sharply with that of those using Gallo-Roman
> and again with that of the Jews, as they each sang his praises in
> their own tongue. 'Long live the King!' they all shouted. 'May
> he continue to reign over his peoples for more years than we can
> count!' The Jews played a full part in these acclamations. 'Let all
> peoples continue to worship you and bow the knee before you and
> submit to your rule!' they kept shouting.[1]

It is also mentioned that the visiting king was invited to
banquets in the houses of the townsfolk, was given gifts by his
hosts 'and gave them presents in return with lavish generosity'.

When some two hundred years earlier St Athanasius
returned to Alexandria after one of his exiles, he was met by
the people as if the Emperor. Everyone poured out of the city;
a day's journey, all pell-mell with all the usual social distinc-
tions swallowed up. Athanasius himself rode a colt, and
people scattered branches, flowers and clothes on his path,
accompanying him back into the city. Everyone was shouting
and cheering, perfumed oils were thrown about, the city was
ablaze with lights, there were banquets everywhere, and the
celebrations went on all night.[2]

Two random, slightly peripheral, examples of an *adventus*.
Other features would be a solemn declamation extolling the
virtues of the monarch, an amnesty for prisoners, handouts for
the people, punishments for any opposition. Interestingly
enough, in the sixth-century West the ceremony attending the
coming of relics to a city was consciously modelled on the
imperial 'advent'.

Certainly, there's hardly a feature of the Advent and Christmas liturgy which can't be 'read' against this background. Think, in general, how prevalent the imagery of kingship is in this liturgy, how the themes of redemption (setting-free) and peace and bestowal run through it. King Guntram enters the houses of the citizens and eats with them. 'Behold I stand at the door and knock; if any one hears my voice and opens the door, I will come in to him and eat with him and he with me' (Rev 3.20). The Son of David comes to the house of bread to eat with us. His advent comes to a climax in the three Masses of Christmas. Or take, in particular, the Gospels of the Genealogy at Christmas Vigils or of the Prologue of John at the Christmas Day Mass. This is the equivalent of the solemn declamation in the presence of the Emperor. 'And the Word became flesh and dwelt among us, full of grace and truth; we have beheld his glory, glory as of the only Son from the Father' (Jn 1.14). In these two Gospels, the first and last of Christmas Day, our Emperor is hailed as son of Abraham, son of David, son of a virgin, son of God the Father. Again, in Orleans the locals and the Syrians and the Jews go out to meet the King with acclamations: Long live the King! The acclamation, the swift sharp shout, was a great part of court life. 'To him who sits upon the throne and to the Lamb be blessing and honour and glory and might for ever and ever' (Rev 5.13) is such transposed to the heavenly court. But take the *Gloria*, the Christmas hymn: *Laudamus te, benedicimus te, adoramus te, glorificamus te . . . Domine Deus, Rex coelestis, Deus pater omnipotens . . . Quoniam tu solus sanctus, tu solus Dominus, tu solus Altissimus Iesus Christe* (literally, 'We praise you, we bless you, we worship you, we glorify you . . . Lord God, Heavenly King, God the omnipotent Father . . . For you alone are holy, you alone are Lord, you alone are the Most High Jesus Christ'). These are our acclamations of the Father and the Son.

The *Adventus* then makes one approach to the next five or six weeks. The paradox, of course, is that at the heart of this State Visit is not a deified superman, a *divus Augustus*, but a little boy born in a barn or, if you prefer, a God who hides himself, whose splendour is humility, and who asks us to become children in turn. When Peter Maxwell Davies remarked, 'I always imagine the nativity in a deserted Rack-wick house' (i.e. on the island of Hoy in the Orkneys), he seems, to us, nearer the heart of things than imperial ceremonial. This coming is a coming-down, and a coming-down which will go on down to a cross and even on down to 'hell'. As the courtier said to Louis XVI, 'This isn't a revolt, Sire, it's a revolution.' It's a very different *imperium* that's coming into being. And yet the liturgy's sense of regality is precisely what preserves and points the paradox.

Secondly, Advent/Christmas is light rising in darkness. It falls at the darkest time of the year. Christmas is kept on the ancient day celebrating the birth of the unconquered Sun, four days after the winter solstice. 'The people who walked in darkness have seen a great light; those who dwelt in a land of deep darkness, on them has light shined' (Is 9.2). *Lux fulgebit hodie super nos* ... 'Radiant light will shine upon us today'. A great light has come down upon the earth. The Masses of Christmas, midnight, dawn and day, celebrate the rising of the true Light. 'Through the mystery of the incarnate Word the new light of your glory has shone on the eyes of our mind,' says Christmas Preface I, and at Epiphany the mystery of our salvation is revealed as the light of the nations, the enlightening of the Gentiles. At Easter we celebrate new *Life*, at Pentecost *Love*, at Christmas *Light*.

Thirdly, Advent-Christmas, this Coming of the King, this dawning of the Light, is also a return from Exile. If Lent recalls the Exodus, God's first great deed on behalf of Israel, Advent recalls the end of the Babylonian captivity, the re-gathering of the tribes, the coming-home to Jerusalem, God's second great deed on behalf of his people. The Anglican historian of Christian origins, N. T. Wright, situates Jesus' life, ministry, death and resurrection precisely within this context: that of first-century Israel's continuing hope for the definitive return from exile, the final restoration. In the language of the Second Christmas Preface, all things are restored to integrity by way of the Incarnation and man, who was lost, is called back to the heavenly realms. There is a reconciliation of Gentile and Jew and a re-building of Jerusalem, that is, the Church. This explains why the Advent/Christmas liturgy is so full of the second half of Isaiah, speaking as it does of this return, this restoration. 'Comfort, comfort my people, says your God. Speak tenderly to Jerusalem and cry to her that her warfare is ended, that her iniquity is pardoned' (Is 40.1–2). This is why Advent-Christmas is always a call to concord, to the reconciliation of the dispersed, to a family life, in home or monastery, centred on Christ and lived in peace.

Notes
1. St Gregory of Tours, *History of the Franks* VIII, 1.
2. Cf. St Gregory Nazianzen, *Discourse* XXI, 29.

5

Christmas Eve

'Hasten! Don't delay, Lord Jesus! Let those who trust in your love, be relieved by the consolations of your coming!' What a prayer this is! One of the very few Collects of the year directly addressed to Jesus himself. Expressing the Church's longing – hunger and ache, holy impatience – for the coming of Christ.

With certainty too. Christ *is* coming. *Hodie scietis.* 'Today you will know ...' And in the coming Christmas season, we will hear about him in words; we will see him, his image in the crib, his image in the Host; we will touch him and taste him. He comes to our spiritual senses, opening them to himself. And because he comes so powerfully, at this time, in word and image and sacrament, because he is truly born for us by way of the rites we celebrate, then our whole time becomes sanctified time, and so we know he will come to us too in our personal reading and prayer, in the movement of our hearts, in the 'good cheer' we have together, in all the kindnesses that people outside the community lavish on us at this time of year. All of this is Christ's birth too. It is an anomaly that the word 'Advent' has slipped into denoting the time of preparation. Today, more rigorously, as the Collect implies, is Advent Eve, the Eve of his Coming. When we enter the Church for the Mass of the Epiphany we will be singing the imperial Introit, *Ecce advenit.* 'Behold, he is coming!' If we have, like citizens of an ancient city, run out to meet our Emperor, *in occursum Domini*, well, the meeting is now. And our Emperor, scattering his bounty, is leading us back into the city. And who, as St Athanasius remarks, would dare attack a city which the Emperor is visiting? Even, we can add, if this Emperor is a child.

So, Christ is coming. And he is coming to us, to our small brotherhood. He is coming to each of us, to me. Coming with consolations. And what do we expect? What do I expect? What consolations do we look for? Beyond the tension and temper of the season, beyond the element of weariness and 'heard it all before', what do we expect? What would it be culpable sloth and sadness not to expect? I offer as an answer something familiar, something true. 'And now faith, hope and love abide, these three; and the greatest of these is love' (1 Cor 13.13). This is the balm Christ brings to ravaged souls. We can expect, each of us can expect – through the celebration of Christ's *Adventus* – a revival of our faith and our hope and our love.

Christmas revives our faith, first of all. Historically, the Christmas liturgy is deeply linked to the great Christological debates of the fourth and fifth centuries, and their resolution in the first ecumenical Councils. As the Byzantine churches instituted a feast of Orthodoxy to hail the defeat of the iconoclasts in the eighth century, so the whole Church was already celebrating Christmas as a proclamation of the full divinity and humanity of Christ, in repudiation of all false doctrine. 'An amazing mystery is proclaimed today: natures are changed: God has become a man: he remains what he was, and he has assumed what he was not: suffering neither mingling nor confusion.' That Benedictus antiphon of the octave day of Christmas only explicates a spirit that runs throughout: a spirit of certain and joyful proclamation. 'To you is born this day in the city of David a Saviour, who is the Messiah, the Lord' (Lk 2.11). What the angel announces, 'evangelizes', at the Mass of midnight, first the Prologue of the Letter to the Hebrews and then the Prologue to the Gospel of John bring to sonorous climax at the day Mass: 'But in these last days, he has spoken to us by a Son, whom he appointed heir of all things, through whom he also created the world. He is the reflection of God's glory and the exact imprint of God's very being' (Heb 1.2–3); 'and the Word became flesh and dwelt among us' (Jn 1.14). It is this newborn child, sleeping or snuffling in the manger, this child who on the eighth day will be called Jesus, who is all these, and other, astonishing things. It's hard not to cry out as the liturgy does at a baptism: 'This is our faith. This is the faith of the Church. We are proud to profess it.'

And so our own faith can be reborn, revitalized, refreshed; our own appreciation of Jesus; our own realization of Jesus. Faith, in this sense, is seeing what the Father sees. Faith is a participation in the mind, in the vision of the Father. That is why Christian faith is so centred on Jesus: because the Father is centred on his Son, eternally and infinitely. Beautiful it is, truly inspired, that the midnight Mass should open as it does with the Introit: *Dominus dixit ad me: Filius meus es tu, ego hodie genui te.* 'The Lord said to me: You are my Son, today have I begotten you.' Christmas begins with the Father addressing the Son, or, strictly, with the Son repeating the word the Father has spoken. Christmas opens with the Father gazing at the baby in the crib, and proclaiming him – as he will at the Jordan and on Tabor and at Easter – his beloved Son, begotten now as man as well as God. 'No one knows the Son except the Father ...' 'Blessed are you, Simon son of Jonah! For flesh and blood has not revealed this to you, but my Father in heaven' (Mt 11.27; 16.17). All true knowledge of the Son comes from heaven, comes from the Father of lights, and our believing will be refreshed and rekindled as we allow the eyes of the Father to look Christ-ward through us. 'Everyone who has heard and learned from the Father comes to me' (Jn 6.45). Faith is seeing what the Father sees.

So can faith see anything other than the Son? Take ourselves. When the Father looks at us, this monastic community, what does he see? He sees us many and one in Christ. He sees, in the grace of the monk, Christ crucified and risen. He sees, in his consecration and obedience, Christ given over to his will, Christ the lover of the Church. He sees Christ the Psalmist, Christ in prayer, Christ celebrating the Passover, Christ reading the Scriptures. He sees Christ the twelve-year-

old in the novice, listening and asking questions. He sees
Christ the teacher in the novice master, Christ the priest and
preacher in the hebdomadary, Christ absolving in the confes-
sor, Christ the shepherd in the oblate master, Christ the
deacon in the cellarer, Christ the healer in the infirmarian,
Christ the host in the guest master, Christ the worker of
Nazareth in the brethren about their ordinary chores, main-
taining the vehicles, counting the money, doing the shopping,
turning the soil. He sees Christ struggling with temptation and
the demons in the desert, Christ overwhelmed at Gethsemane,
Christ in tears sometimes, Christ disconsolate, Christ weary
in the old. In the measure our faith is revived at Christmas,
so will we see too – with the eyes of the Father. 'Even the
darkness is not dark to you.' These eyes will even light up our
inner selves. *Dixit dominus ad me: Filius meus es tu: ego
hodie genui te.* 'This is my Son [too] the Beloved; my favour
rests on him.' No one on earth, nothing in history, nothing in
contemporary events, nothing in the story of my life isn't
under this gaze of the Father, isn't therefore full of Christ,
even if it's Christ rejected or Christ wrapped in the stone cold
tomb awaiting the touch of the Father. Christmas shows us
Christ. Christmas revives our faith.

Christmas revives our hope. Every newborn child has that
power; this Child uniquely. He revives, first, the hope of a
better world here and now, of a change for the good. His birth
coincides with the lengthening days. It gives fresh energy in
the doing of good: ordinary, daily, mundane good. It sends us
out to battle once again. Our sense of it all being somehow
worth it finds itself strangely rekindled by that Mother and
Child. 'For all that loveliness, that warmth, that light,/Blessed
Madonna, I go back to fight', wrote a great British general in
1943 (Lord Wavell). He revives the hope, looking higher, of
the Kingdom to come. He's already a fulfilment, by way of
cross and resurrection, of the hopes of the Chosen People:
those hopes of God reigning and idols toppling, of a new
covenant, of a gathered people and Gentiles converted, of a
new Presence, of a new purity and inward renewal, of the

forgiveness of sins, of the Messianic king. All these promises have a first, unfinished but real, fulfilment in the Church and in her saints. Seeing this much, as St Augustine says, our hope is revived in the ultimate happy ending. He revives our hope, thirdly, personally, for heaven. In the Collect for Christmas night, we pray to 'enjoy in heaven the joys of him whose luminous mysteries we celebrate on earth.' The best is yet to come, for each of us.

There is a key. It's to be deeply, inwardly convinced of being personally loved by the Lord. This is what withers fear and stirs up hope. The Holy Spirit will show each one of us how to decipher the script of our life in the light of Christ's love. My Christian baptism, my being or becoming a Catholic, the Eucharist, my vocation, my ordination if such, the work I've been given, the people I know – even my infirmities – these are all of them the words of Christ's love in my life. And the last and best of the words, the word to illuminate everything, completing the sentence in unimaginable fullness and joy, is still to come. It's the word of my final salvation, the word of eternal life, the word: 'Your sins are forgiven'; the word: 'Well done, good and faithful servant, enter into the joy of your Lord.' And strange though it may seem, it is the hope of that word that this Child brings. It's the hope of birth into bliss. Christmas revives our hope.

Christmas revives our love. According to the doctrine of what is called the hypostatic union, Christ's human nature – which is completely like ours, sin excepted (and sin is not a part of nature) – belongs as his own to the divine person of the Son of God, who assumed it. In other words, one of the Trinity has made a human nature part of himself. This is love, overwhelming, mind-blowing, heart-ravishing love. This is love than which no greater can be conceived. There is a being, God, who is completely, infinitely, eternally, unassailably happy, blessed, joyful, in his own Trinitarian life. This Being decides, out of love, to create other, finite beings outside itself, centrally man, in order to share its happiness with them. And when it does this, it does it to the maximum conceivable,

even though or even because, the human creature has refused
the love. One of the Trinity in order to connect to each and
every man takes to himself an individual human nature in a
marriage than which there is no closer or more intimate.
Humanity is part of the Trinity: indissolubly and forever. By
taking a human nature to himself, the Son of God has united
himself in a certain way to every human being. Christ is part
of every human's humanity, more me than I am. Really, a
clatter of genuflections at the *Et incarnatus est* hardly rises to
the occasion! I only mention what most immediately aston-
ishes me: this act of Incarnation, God marrying humanity. But
then there's the child, the teacher, the suffering One, the risen
One, the One who gives the Spirit, the One who breaks the
bread of his Body. They all speak the same love, and they are
all, in the unity of his Person, one and the same, and present
already at Christmas.

The only possible knock-on effect – though heaven knows
how many Christmasses it takes to come to it – is St Benedict's enlarged heart. The heart of the Trinity is large enough
for all humanity. Alas, at times I can find my own family and
brethren too much of a squeeze. But what is it after all that
the Lord wants of the monk? What is the goal of all his
famous 'trials' if not that kind of heart? Not actions or auster-
ities or prayers or achievements in themselves, but a wider
heart, a heart widened by the Christmas love.

'Hasten! Don't delay, Lord Jesus! Let those who trust in your
love be relieved by the consolations of your coming.' 'Faith,
hope and love; these three abide.' Cold comfort? Yes, in a
sense, but, in a truer sense, anything but. Faith, hope and
love: they are the balm; they are the sustenance; they are the
consolation. They bind us to God and they bind us to one
another. They complete the incarnation. They are the sign of
his birth in our souls. They bring us to the childhood which
is salvation. They keep us going till he comes in glory.

6

Adoration

'We have seen his star in the East and have come to worship him' (Mt 2.2). Every mystery of Christ has a power and a grace of its own, a gift of the Spirit, and every liturgical celebration of every mystery enables us to receive that and be changed by it, 'inwardly reshaped' as one of the Christmas prayers says. What is the power and the grace of the Epiphany, the manifestation of the Lord? One answer is adoration.

The Magi are the patron saints and pioneers of Christian adoration. 'And going into the house they saw the child with Mary his mother, and they fell down and worshipped him (*adoraverunt eum*)' (Mt 2.11). The Introits and other chants in the Roman Gradual for the first few weeks of the year keep coming back to this *adoratio*. With the Magi, specifically Christian worship begins. No wonder that this moment, like the moment of the Annunciation, has inspired so much Christian art. We are all invited to adore in the wake of these wise men. We do so fulfilling the prophecy of Psalm 71.11: 'May all kings fall down before him'; obeying Psalm 28, 'worship the Lord in his holy court', and Psalm 94, 'O come let us worship and bow down, let us kneel before the Lord our Maker.' We are imitating the angels, who are busy obeying God's command, as he brings the firstborn into the world, 'Let all God's angels worship him' (Heb 1.6). And more: when we follow the Magi in adoring, we are also following all those who, throughout the Gospel of Matthew, do what the Magi did (the leper, a ruler, the disciples, the Canaanite woman, the mother of James and John, and climactically, after the Resurrection, the women at the tomb and the eleven disciples on the mountain in Galilee). And finally: we are anticipating and sharing in the heavenly worship of God and the Lamb so central to the Apocalypse.

'We have come to worship him'; 'Come, let us adore him!' The gift of Epiphany is rediscovering adoration.

What does 'to adore' mean? What is the sense of its Latin roots? Etymologically, to turn the mouth (*os*) towards (*ad*), and so to speak to, to address; thence, to speak to someone in order to obtain something, especially a deity; to beseech, implore; thence, dropping the idea of asking and entreating, to reverence, honour, adore, worship the gods. It is more emphatic than *venerari*, to honour, and denotes the highest degree of reverence, equivalent to the Greek *proskunein*, to prostrate. So there is something ultimate to adoration. It is as far as we can go. Even when I say, 'I adore mushroom soup' or 'I adore my little sister', I am, at one level anyway, saying something strong. 'To love deeply' is the first meaning of 'adore' given in the dictionary. We can bless God, praise him, glorify him, as in the *Gloria* of the Mass, but when we 'adore' him we do, it seems, take a further step. We go as far as we can go. The closest equivalent is 'worship', with its Old English roots and its sense of acknowledging worth. It often does duty translating the Latin or the Greek, as for the action of the Magi. It is, though, rather less sharply-focused than 'adoration'.

If 'ultimacy' is one resonance of adoring, being bodily is another. 'And they *fell down* and worshipped.' Adoring and falling down, adoring and prostrating, adoring and hitting the ground: they go together. *Proskynesis* and *adoratio* were used for this physical showing of homage to emperors and kings and high officials. In the story of the Magi, it finds its true destination at last: Christ, the true King. Man is on his knees or on his face before the true Epiphany of the divine. The whole battle of the first three Christian centuries will turn on this: Whom do we adore? Who is worthy of worship? To whom do we bend the knee?

Often paintings of the Adoration – not only of the kings, but of the shepherds and/or Mary and Joseph – evoke this falling down. The child is low, even on the floor, and one king is already on his knees before him, the next one stooping, the last still standing. And so the eye and the beholder are drawn into this movement of falling down and worshipping. And then comes the reflection that this movement is merely answering the downward movement of the Incarnation itself.

Adoration is 'first'. It's primary; it's a foundation. It is the *first* commandment: 'You shall have no strange gods before me.' As Dom Denis Huerre wrote, 'The first step to adoration is away from the "many words" of idolators, away from their *multiloquio* toward the soberness (*nepsis*) or "fewness of words", which Benedict indicates to be the opposite of the chattering world of gossip'.[1] Is this why it features so prominently at the beginning of the liturgical year? At the beginning of each liturgical day by way of Psalm 94? At the beginning of the Lord's Prayer, 'Hallowed be thy name'?

To adore, says the *Catechism*, is 'to acknowledge', to acknowledge God 'as God, as the Creator and Saviour, the Lord and Master of everything that exists, as infinite and merciful Love' (2096). 'It is homage of the spirit to the King of Glory, respectful silence in the presence of the "ever-greater" God' (2628). It is entering the Temple. At the same time, it is acknowledging the 'nothingness of the creature', humbling oneself like Mary. 'I am reduced to nothing' before the One who makes me and rescues me.

So, finally, it is liberating – from idolatry of the world, from turning in upon oneself. I read the other day that of the two most widespread modern sins, 'narcissism' (self-contemplation, self-absorption) is the first. Adoration rescues us from that. It heals.

So we can follow the Magi. 'We have come to adore him.' Adoration begins Matthew's Gospel, and completes it. 'And behold Jesus met them – Mary Magdalene and the other Mary – and said, "Rejoice!" And they came up and took hold of his feet and worshipped him' (Mt 28.9). And a few verses later: 'Now the eleven disciples went to Galilee, to the mountain to which Jesus had directed them. And when they saw him, they worshipped him; but some doubted' (28.16–17).

But let us explore a little more. Islam visibly, five times a day, worships the one, transcendent God, humbling himself to the ground. But what provokes the adoration of the Magi, *Christian* adoration? It is the mystery of God's self-humbling, it is the Epiphany of God in the flesh, the coming of Christ, the God-man. What calls forth Christian adoration is, in this sense (the sense of the incarnation), an epiphany, a manifestation, a vision of glory. It is the glory of God shining on the face of Christ. 'Where is he who has been *born* King of the Jews?' (Mt 2.2). He is born from Mary's womb and the Magi adore. He rises from the empty tomb, and the two Marys and eleven disciples adore. He presents himself to their vision, they *see* him, they adore. 'And going into the house they *saw* the child with Mary, his mother, and they fell down and worshipped him.' 'And when they – the eleven – *saw* him, they worshipped him.' It's the same in the Gospel of John. 'Do you believe in the Son of Man?' Jesus asks the man born blind, now seeing. 'And who is he, sir, that I may believe in him?' 'Jesus said to him, "You have *seen* him, and it is he who speaks to you." He said, "Lord, I believe", and he worshipped him' (Jn 9.35–38).

Christian adoration is a response to God revealing himself in Christ. It is a Spirit-given recognition of the glory of God the Father shining on the face of Christ. Where, we then wonder, is this epiphany to be found, this well-spring of adoration.

First of all in the Christian liturgy. When the cantor begins the *Gloria Patri*, says St Benedict, 'let them all rise up immediately from honour and reverence for the Holy Trinity' (*Rule* 9.7). We rise to bow. It's as if the three divine names, Father, Son and Holy Spirit, are in themselves an epiphany and bring us to adoration. Liturgy is epiphany, the epiphany of the Trinity in the economy of the Incarnation. Liturgy is the house we enter to discover Mary, his mother, and the Child. Everything in the liturgy is a sign, everything holds and yields its secret of divine light. The church building itself and its furnishings, the altar especially; the assembly gathered to worship, an epiphany of Christ's body the Church; the presiding priesthood; the order of ritual; the word of God, the Scriptures proclaimed and sung; the sacramental action; the Eucharist itself supremely, the hidden but radiant Epiphany in the House of Bread, *the* sacramental focus of adoration beyond all others. Nothing has such power to 're-arrange' us, that is, our priorities, as adoration of the Blessed Sacrament. All of this is a school for, and already a participation in, the eternal celestial worship of the Lamb 'in the midst of the Throne'.

But then we know how anxious St Benedict is for integrity. 'Before you call on me,' says the Lord – outside the liturgy, therefore, as well as inside it – 'I will say to you, "Here I am"' (Prologue 18). 'We *believe*,' he says, 'that the divine presence is everywhere' (*Rule* 19.1); therefore the divine epiphany; therefore the opportunity for adoration. At Compline each night we have another day's reasons for agreeing with Simeon: 'my eyes have seen your salvation'. 'At the work of God, in the oratory, in the garden, on the path, in the field, or anywhere' (7.63), the monk can be seeing God, adoring God 'in spirit and in truth'. 'To be perpetually aware of the presence of God is to be perpetually aware of his glory, and it is this awareness that makes every word and every gesture (all that we say and do) an act of adoration.'[2]

If for the monk the liturgy is one school of adoration, the virtue, or rather, the experience, the grace of humility is another. There's no essential difference, after all.

'I am reduced to nothing.' St Benedict quotes that psalm phrase on the sixth of his twelve steps of humility. Is it not the centre and the key of the whole business? 'You shall worship the Lord your God and him only shall you serve' (Mt 4.10). The monk is someone who does one thing only, *that* one thing. And when he is reduced to nothing, then he's on the threshold of adoration. The epiphany of God can come by way of its opposite. I remember from Andre Maurois' autobiography how on the day France fell in 1940, he, in England, flung himself on a bed and lay there for hours. It's the prostration of Gethsemane. Events, tragedies, the actions of others can reduce us to nothing, make us literally unable to speak, throw us to the ground, bring us down to the dust, like Saul of Tarsus outside Damascus. And that can be the birth of adoration. The idols fall; the gods we looked for for life fall: our competence or position or knowledge or popularity or friendships or reputation or just our things. And we fall back, anguished, into the great black hole of our nothingness. If, by faith, we realize God is showing himself in his glory precisely then; if we can be 'content' with being unloved and marginalized or whatever it is; then our nothingness becomes a runway up – or down – to adoration. The stars must have lost their divinity for their Magi, their whole life in one sense falling into nothingness, but they recognized the sun in the child on Mary's lap. In the moments when our world collapses, may we discover the God beyond all things.

There is too, I think, the adoration of exhaustion. There's nothing left in me. All I can do is throw myself down and worship. No other prayer but my body. But that'll do.

The Epiphany in the liturgy, the Epiphany in my nothingness. To be whole, as St Benedict would wish, we must add the Epiphany in the other, in the brother or sister. Christ is to be adored in the guests who are welcomed, says the *Rule*, 'head bowed or the whole body prostrate on the ground' (53.7). And not in guests only . . .

Many the ways then the Epiphany can come. The modality matters little. The thing is to see and respond as the Magi did. 'And they fell down and worshipped him.'

Every mystery brings its gift of the Spirit, the Epiphany, it seems, that of adoration. It's a gift we can ask for. It's a gift very right for beginning a year, especially one capable of bringing some terrible things. If we can carry away sentiments of adoration, all our liturgy and meditation won't have been wasted. The Magi must have carried their adoration for the rest of their lives. The Church, in their wake, is perpetually adoring. So are the angels. 'On a high throne I saw a man sitting, and a host of angels adoring.' It is always Epiphany, always time to adore.

Notes
1. Abbot Denis Huerre, *Letters to my Brothers and Sisters* (Liturgical Press, Princeton, New Jersey, 1994), pp. 57–58.
2. Ibid., p. 61.

7

Water and the Spirit

What a blessing the liturgical year is! It's such a support for
personal spiritual life, for prayer. All day, every day, various
thoughts and feelings ebb and flow within us. The Desert
Fathers talk of the fish swimming in the water. We're in the
boat of ourselves and we look down into the water: at our
thoughts and emotions. Which are better forgotten? Which are
worth hauling in? We need to discern, and discernment needs
criteria. And I think the liturgical year is a criterion, it can
help us discern. In other words, there may be a current of
thought running through us, a line developing. And we
suddenly realize: ah yes, this connects with where we are
liturgically, with the season, with a feast, with what we're
hearing read to us. And that can be a confirmation. The Holy
Spirit is here. I'm reading Sigrid Undset's *Kristin Lavrans-
datter* at the moment, the story of this (imaginary) fourteenth-
century Norwegian woman, and her connections. And it all
unfolds, discreetly and tellingly all at once, against the background of the Church's year. The liturgy sets the underlying
rhythm. It establishes a whole series of hidden connections. It
gives a depth. And so, in our little world, with us. A farmer
or a gardener never has to spend an inordinate amount of time
deciding what he's going to do next: the seasons do that for
him. And so with our praying: the liturgical round, daily,
weekly, yearly, pours into our lap possibilities of prayer,
means of approach to the Lord. This has been said often, I'm
sure, but maybe it bears repetition. We're carried in our
prayer. Our subconscious life is acted upon by the liturgy.

And when what comes to the surface in our minds and hearts chimes with what's ringing in the liturgical air, we can be at peace, we can feel confirmed.

Christmas we all find tiring, but at another level how it energizes! When Our Lord came out from the baptismal waters, he came out, surely, breathing fire. The Spirit 'drove' him into the wilderness, according to St Mark, into spiritual warfare. And after the desert war, according to St Luke, Jesus returned to Galilee 'in the power of the Spirit'. This is the Spirit that came on him at his baptism. And maybe our Christmas effort can revive the Spirit who came upon us at our baptism and confirmation. St Francis de Sales speaks of 'gathering a bouquet' after times of prayer: gathering together the good 'things' we feel may have happened, the good thoughts, the good inspirations. And I think it's good, as one liturgical phase comes to an end, to do something like that: not just to drift unreflectingly from one thing to the next. There are graces of incarnation offered at Christmas: acceptance of life as it is because God is in it and God lives beyond it as its goal. Perhaps the thought of life without Christ becomes that bit more unthinkable. Perhaps we feel we belong more. Perhaps there has been a growth in peace. Perhaps more sense of the *mysterium* of Colossians, 'Christ in you, the hope of glory' (Col 1.27), of God at work in the world. Perhaps more love of the brother whom we can see, following 1 John, a vision of God at work in the other. Perhaps more love of and commitment to the Church, the bride Christ comes in search of. And so on. Surely something rubs off, even if we cannot name it. It may be no more than an almost imperceptible sense of something good being born in us.

Now just to sketch of a line of thought inspired by the imminent feast of the Lord's Baptism. At Jesus' baptism we see the two things that comprise our own: water and the Spirit. And since baptism is a new birth – 'truly, truly, I say to you, unless one is born of water and the Spirit, he cannot enter the

kingdom of God' (Jn 3.5) – it is possible for a preacher like
Maximus of Turin to speak of Christ being 'born for men' at
Christmas and 'reborn in/for the sacraments' at Epiphany.
'Then he was brought forth by the Virgin; today he is brought
forth through a mystery.' He is saying that, as at Christmas
Jesus' life on earth began, so at the Baptism his life in the
Church began: he is born in us through our rebirth in baptism.
On that day he consecrated the waters, as the Fathers say; he
instituted the sacrament of baptism, as the Scholastics would
say.

Water and the Spirit: new birth. There's much meaning
hidden here. This new birth has the features of the old, and
transforms the old. We are all born from, so to say, the water
of a mother and the spirit of a father. Now we are reborn of
the sacramental water given power by the Spirit of God. The
font is a womb, made fertile by the Spirit. Water suggests the
mother – Mary – the Church. We are born, we become sons
of the Father, through the twofold action of the Church and
the Holy Spirit. The world itself came to be 'from water and
the Spirit', according to Genesis (1.2). As a matter of biolog-
ical fact, life, which is impossible without a special interven-
tion of the Holy Spirit, came out of water. We begin to
glimpse the extraordinary unity of God's plan.

And there's more, too. We are what we are – not merely
bodily, but at the level of temperament and personality –
thanks to our parents and family. We spring from that water.
The older we get the more – famously! – we see our parents
in ourselves. Our general social background, our culture:
that's part of the water too; so is our education, and any
professional formation we've had. But above all, our parents,
our family. St Matthew begins his Gospel with Jesus' genealogy; a tribute to this truth. It is there that attitudes and ways
of behaviour were formed. It was there, in fact, that we were
simultaneously formed and deformed and, please God, first
reformed. If I pause on the de-formed, it's not to overlook all
the good we've received from our parents (a good we can
never adequately repay), but because, paradoxically, the deformed will be above all where God's glory is seen.

Let's be old-fashioned and say that what is deformed

surfaces as 'passions', that is, irrational, disordered desires. Perhaps we can name our particular 'ruling passion'. Where does it come from? Desires spring from needs. I desire food because I need food. I want (in the sense of desire) because I want (in the sense of lack). Unregulated desires spring from unregulated needs. And where do the hungry, cavernous, chaotic needs come from? From father Adam and mother Eve: from human nature as fallen, as deformed. But they take their particular configuration in me because of what I underwent and reacted to as a child. Take, for example, the need to be noticed, to be a centre of attention. It can be very strong; it can colour vast areas of life and behaviour. It's a disorder, a passion, a de-formation needing reformation. But where does it come from? Surely from early, familial, domestic experience, perhaps from some anguishing moment of neglect, from a sudden 'baptism' in unhallowed water.

One is wary of the jeremiad, of course, not to mention the shifting of blame. We know every family in history, even Our Lord's extended family, has been dysfunctional – this from father Adam and mother Eve onwards. (I'll spare you Philip Larkin's much-quoted line!) We know, too, creation is continuing, that 'the generative forces of the world are wholesome' (Wis 1.14), that 'there lives the dearest freshness deep down things', that even some of those working with the unspeakably abused can talk of 'resilience', that grace is always at its healing work. But still, it's not unreasonable to anticipate that the contemporary breakdown of family in the Western world will have (is having) vast psychological and behavioural consequences. Anyone working in the area of formation in religious life, for example, would confirm that. There can be a new level of difficulty in people's lives, a new density of pain, a new depth of 'deformation'. A need, in consequence, for a vast, deep, soul-searching reformation, for what some call 're-parenting'.

Water and the Holy Spirit. Is there not an opportunity here, such as never before, for the Church and the Spirit? If a great cry is going up for re-formation of heart, soul and mind, it is, we could say, a cry for a healing water and a Holy Spirit. And these, since Our Lord went down into the Jordan and hallowed the waters, to come up under the life-giving Dove, these exist. A spring has been opened. There is another water now – Mary, the Church, the sacraments, the liturgy – into which our deformity can be plunged and the reforming grace of the Holy Spirit be received. Immersed in such waters we can be healed, like Naaman of his leprosy. We can be reformed of our deformity (much of this happening, surely, at the subconscious and unconscious levels – levels where the liturgy and grace can work with ease). This is why, incidentally, our times call for liturgies of meaning, power and beauty. The salvation of souls is at stake.

Water and the Spirit. 'I', this means, is not what I am simply by my first birth. 'I' is not what I am as a result of my past, my Adamic past, my family past, my past life. 'I' – the true I – is 'hidden with Christ in God', where Christ is seated at the right hand of the Father; it is in the future. My truth, my identity, is in my membership of the body of the risen Christ. And as yet I hardly have a notion of it. How unnecessary, though, to limit, define, imprison myself by, identify myself with, what my childhood made of me and I of it! Adam and my whole personal genealogy has had an immense influence upon me, it is true, total in fact. And none of that, good or bad, is to be denied, but it is all to be changed. I need not be prisoner of it, or slave to it, condemned to toil away for ever at the tasks given by my conditioning, my neuroses, my past sins. 'All things are yours, and you are Christ's, and Christ is God's' (1 Cor 3.22–23). The power of Christ and Church, the power of the Spirit and the sacraments is infinitely greater, infinitely more life-giving, infinitely liberating, however secret their work, however disconcerting their rhythms, however arduous the restoration, in practice, of my freedom. This is the mystery of the forgiveness of sins, rebirth, re-creation, of the working out of the grace of baptism. It's the healing touch of Christ. Formed by creation, deformed by sin, I am to be reformed by grace, transformed in glory.

Forgive me for expressing this so clumsily. Perhaps I simply want to say this: that in the 'waters' of Mary's motherhood, of the Church, her liturgy, her sacraments, her baptism, the restorative, life-giving energy of the Spirit is at work; that thanks to this Spirit, a new birth, a new bringing-forth, a re-formation, a new education, a new beginning is possible. 'A new creation rises from the River', proclaims one antiphon from our feast: Jesus Christ who comes up from the waters of the Jordan with the Spirit upon him, and we too, born again by water and the Spirit. This new creation is more than, greater than, the old. The corrupt and defective in the latter, in our past, it heals and turns to good; the inherited goodness, it retains, and raises to new levels. 'Behold, I make all things new' (Rev 21.5), beginning from this baptism. Perhaps, most simply, it comes down to what Elisha once said to his servant: 'Fear not, for those who are with us are more than those who are with them' (2 Kings 6.16), and to what St John wrote in his First Letter: 'Little children, you are of God, and have overcome them [the spirits which do not confess Jesus]; for he who is in you is greater than he who is in the world' (1 Jn 4.4).

8

The Conversion of Flesh

God having made us the way we are, what does the body mean
to us? How important should it be for us? The first thing to make
clear is that we cannot answer such questions unless we think of
ourselves as living human beings, not bits of things stuck
together, whether we talk of two things (body and mind) or three
things (mind, body, heart). We are not an assembly of parts, but
integral units or entities. There cannot be a true spirituality unless
it expresses the whole of what we are. Benedictines have been
celebrated for the equilibrium in which our monasteries keep
body and spirit; yet there are some tendencies today that seem to
forget this and tie labels on monks: for example, A is a lay
brother type, B is an intellectual type, C is an artistic type etc.
What these labels do is deny people the possibility of developing
their other human aspects and becoming that ideal Benedictine
that is the balanced human . . .

The heart, spirit or deep centre is what helps us to live so that
'flesh' is constantly being converted into 'body' . . . Flesh needs
conversion into body . . .[1]

I

Dom Denis Huerre, a former Abbot of La Pierre-qui-Vire and
Abbot President of the Subiaco Congregation uses the phrase
'the conversion of flesh into body'. That, we can say, is the
purpose of fasting and abstinence, of physical mortification, of
asceticism. Not the destruction or weakening of the body, but
a beginning of its redemption. Not a disregard for the body,

but a realization of our responsibility for it. Yes, I am responsible for my body.

For many people, their body is a source of shame and embarrassment; or again, a source of a rather ridiculous vanity. It can mean pain or pleasure. It can have been the object of abuse or an agent of violence, or both. It can be a comfortable place or a very uncomfortable one. It's where every human being lives and every human being dies. 'For we are born in others' pain/and perish in our own'.[2]

Many years ago Fr Laurence O'Keeffe of Ramsgate gave us a retreat on the Psalms. What he stressed was 'the Christian meaning of the Psalms'. There is, too, a Christian meaning of the body. It doesn't abolish all other meanings, but it does relativize them. This Christian meaning (and dignity) derives from our union with Christ in his body the Church. If the Church is the body of Christ in the world, our own bodies cannot be irrelevant to that. They must be his, in some sense. They are incorporated into the body of Christ, and so receive a new identity and mission. They receive this at baptism. From that moment, whatever we do and *suffer* in our bodies (death included) takes on a new meaning. We are 'in Christ' also in our bodies.

'Contemplate the face of Christ' was the Pope's word to all the faithful as we enter the third millennium. 'In him,' says St Paul, 'the whole fullness of the deity dwells bodily' (Col 2.19). Christian contemplation is always contemplation of the Word made flesh, of the embodied deity. The Seventh Ecumenical Council is not simply about the validity of iconography. It authorizes the imagination and a Christian cult of the body: the eyes, the face, the form, the hands, of Christ, his mother, the saints. We approach the Godhead only through the flesh of the God-made-man. We contemplate the Christ-child, the Christ-youth, the Christ-man. We hear him speaking; we see him touching the leper; we see him using his spittle to open a pair of eyes. We look at Christ thrown to the ground in the garden, Christ scourged, Christ crowned with thorns, Christ under the Cross and on the Cross and being taken down from the Cross. We contemplate him risen and transfigured. We seek his face. We await his bodily return and our bodily resurrection. All this is our way to the invisible Father. Surely it will modify our view of, our attitude towards human bodies.

When we see a dying man, of whom will we think, of whose body? When we see a mother and child, who come to mind? Caryll Houselander had a famous vision in a London underground train, seeing everyone in Christ (the mystical Body). From that moment she understood just how heinous are the sins of lust. Similarly, sins of violence. Somehow health or strength or fitness or beauty or pleasure can't be the final meanings or purposes of the body, precious though these be. Our perspectives and attitudes start to shift. And if we go on with this contemplation, won't it, unbeknown to us, begin a surreptitious transformation of our own bodies? There is the movement of grace, the trickle-down effect, from spirit to soul to body, or from the heart filled with the Name out to the outermost limbs. Human bodies reflect the work they're put to. A farmer or gardener carries that in his face and his hands and his posture. Similarly the man of prayer. His body will quieten, will acquire a subtle refinement, will unify, may even glow a little.

Add to this the Eucharist, the sacramental body of Christ. St Cyril of Jerusalem famously remarked that, thanks to this mystery, we become 'con-corporeal and con-sanguinary' with Christ. St Irenaeus saw reception of the Eucharist as the hidden source of our ultimate bodily resurrection. Conversely, St Paul attributes certain illnesses and even deaths among the Corinthians to un-discerning, unworthy reception of the body and blood of the Lord (1 Cor 11.27–30). All this implies physical consequences to eating the body and drinking the blood of Christ. Prayer and the sacraments, then, channel the Holy Spirit, and the Holy Spirit works in our bodies as well as our souls.

II

What, then, is this Christian meaning of the body? John Paul II spoke, clarifyingly and in depth, of the 'nuptial meaning' of the body. There are other aspects too, I think. Firstly, the iconic. St Francis de Sales said of it: 'The body of the Christian is an *image* of the incarnate Saviour.' Of itself, the body is an icon or image of the soul, or the spirit, or the person; in Christ, it's an icon of him. Perhaps with the refinement: that the body of a man in Christ images him, of a woman in Christ images the Church, and so Mary. The body is, of course, still 'the body of death', 'dead because of sin', says St Paul (Rom 8.10), that is, still liable to death, and it can always be an icon of whatever is uppermost, for better or worse, in our souls. The body remains a battlefield, where life and death fight out their duel, victory still apparently going to the latter. My body reflects my age, my race, my sex. It can also reflect my exhaustion, my anger, my depression, my *acedia*. That's true. But still, so far as it is a body 'in Christ', a temple of the Spirit, a body destined for resurrection, it can reflect the things of God. 'Christ plays in ten thousand places, lovely in eyes, lovely in limbs not his.'[3]

Secondly, the liturgical. 'I appeal to you therefore, brethren, by the mercies of God, to present your bodies as a living sacrifice, holy and acceptable to God, which is your spiritual worship.' So says St Paul in Romans 12.1. 'So glorify God in your body,' he says in 1 Corinthians 6.20. These are great texts, foundational texts. The body is that by which we make our whole lives a worship of God. The body is made for doxology. This takes us very far from the reductionist philosophies of the human body for sale on the contemporary market. St John Chrysostom has a striking commentary on this verse of Romans:

> How is the body to become a sacrifice? Keep your eye from looking at anything evil, and it has become a sacrifice. Keep your tongue from dirty talk, and it has become an offering. Keep your hand from anything unlawful, and it has become a holocaust. This, though, isn't enough. We must also be engaged in good works. Make your hand give alms, make your mouth bless those who cross you, devote your hearing to the public readings of Scripture. Sacrifice is incompatible with anything unclean, and it is offered as a first-fruits. So let us offer first-fruits to God through our hands and feet and mouth and all our limbs ... Our whole life should be thought of as ministering and serving. And

this will happen if every day you bring him yourself as a sacrifice, and become the priest of your own body ... Each one is a priest of his own flesh by his way of life.[4]

Thirdly, the instrumental. 'I chastise my body and make a slave of it' (1 Cor 9.27). A slave, or a servant, who, as I said, is fit for work, 'a fellow-worker in the service of better things', as St Maximus puts it. 'For just as you once yielded your members to impurity and to greater and greater iniquity, so now yield your members to righteousness for (*eis*) sanctification' (Rom 6.19), admonishes St Paul. Compulsions and addictions clog us or short-circuit us, unfit us for God's purposes. They reduce the body's serviceability. Asceticism is designed to enhance it. It's a process of honing. The true ascetic is like St Paul, someone who can do his work – that is, the Lord's work – in any physical circumstances. 'I have learned in whatever state I am to be content' (Phil 4.11). What a teacher in all this St Paul is! In any case, it is this instrumental, 'diaconal' meaning of the body that explains much of the more fearsome language of Christian tradition: Brother Ass, and so on. What such language simply implies is that the body is called to share in the mission of Christ and the Church. It's an instrument of *service*.

Sacramentally joined to Christ, the human body takes on a new Christian nature. Joined to Christ, it takes on a new beauty, able to reflect the crucified and risen One, its 'iconic meaning'. Joined to Christ, it takes on a new use, 'liturgical' and 'instrumental', all at once dedicated to the worship of God and the service of others.

III

It is Lent – a time for 'the conversion of flesh into body' – and it's good to be practical. If I were to suggest one thing to look at and enhance, it might be bodily posture, and, at the happy risk of anticipating Easter, the posture especially of *standing*. On Good Friday, we'll hear from St John: '*standing* by the Cross of Jesus were his mother, and his mother's sister,

Mary the wife of Clopas, and Mary Magdalene' (Jn 19.25), and every time the Second Eucharistic Prayer is used, we hear: 'we thank you for counting us worthy to *stand* in your presence and serve you.' The Christian, the monk, is called to *stand* by the Cross, to *stand* in the Father's presence. In that posture, a whole life, a whole attitude of soul is condensed.

French monks, at least of our houses, have a habit of standing in prayer before any Office. I was struck by this at a General Chapter of our Congregation. There was a sea of us in church before some Office, all sitting, and among us, like trees rising from a swamp, a scattering of Gallic abbots standing erect. 'God made man upright', says Ecclesiastes (7.29), 'but they have sought out many devices.' Fallen man is *homo incurvatus* ('made crooked or bent'). It is this which gives such symbolic poignancy to the healing of the woman with 'a spirit of infirmity for eighteen years', a daughter of Abraham, bound by Satan, bent over, unable to 'fully straighten herself'. 'And when Jesus saw her, he called her and said to her, "Woman, you are freed from your infirmity." And he laid his hands upon her, and immediately she was made straight, and she praised God' (Lk 13.11–13). She stands again, and she praises. Standing is the primary biblical posture for prayer. 'So the men turned from there, and went toward Sodom; but Abraham still *stood* before the Lord' (Gen 18.22), and standing began his intercession. 'Who shall climb the mountain of the Lord? Who shall *stand* in his holy place?' asks the Psalmist (Ps 23.3). 'O come, bless the Lord, all you who serve the Lord, who *stand* in the house of the Lord, in the courts of the house of our God' (Ps 133.1): the last Psalm of the monastic day. 'And Solomon awoke, and behold it was a dream. Then he came to Jerusalem, and *stood* before the ark of the covenant of the Lord, and offered up burnt offerings and peace offerings ...' (1 Kings 3.15). Standing too is what one might call the patristic position, 'as is clear from the paintings in the catacombs, the sculptures on early sarcophaguses, and the works of the first ecclesiastical writers' (A-G Martimort). It is the major liturgical posture: that of the priest, especially when celebrating the sacrifice at the altar,

that of the faithful at Mass, with the exception of the consecration and where there is a custom of kneeling. It's the
angelic posture, too; angels 'stand' – the Bible imagines –
before God. That's significant. Liturgy is the place where all
the fissures in the universe are healed. One of them is that
between man and angels. If, suddenly, they have the same
posture, they are reconciled. It's the posture of heaven, the
eschatological posture, the end answering to the beginning:
'After this I looked, and behold a great multitude which no
man could number, from every nation, from all tribes and
peoples and tongues, *standing* before the throne and before the
Lamb' (Rev 7.9). It is, of course, also the posture of Sunday
and Eastertide, the paschal posture. We kneel for the *Angelus*,
we stand for the *Regina Caeli*.

It is also the posture, in St Benedict's mind, for psalmody
(*Rule* 19.7). For listening (the Gospel aside), there is sitting
(9.5); for praying (that is, after the Psalms) kneeling or prostrating (20.5; 50.3). But for psalmody itself, monks stand. All
sorts of concessions have been made here to human comfort.
So we sit for the psalmody of Vigils and recline for all other
psalmody. Is that a gain? We talk of St Benedict's balance,
and most of Benedictine history has consisted in variously
upsetting it. St Benedict's monks would have stood for so
many hours at psalmody, would have sat for some hours for
lectio, would normally have moved and used their bodies at
manual work, and lain down at night and at siesta time. There
is balance and completeness. Now, are we so different from
someone with his armchair at home, his car to work, his easy
chair in the office?

An excessively sedentary culture induces excessively sedentary prayer, a reduction of the Christian use of the body.
There is indeed a time for sitting; it is the posture for listening, especially. 'King David went in and sat before the Lord'
(2 Sam 7.18), pondering the astonishing promises conveyed
by the prophet Nathan. But there is a time for standing too,
and Tradition is very much on its side. Why stand, then? It's
a sign of respect; we stand in the presence of one we wish to
honour. It's acknowledging that someone greater is there. It is
fear of the Lord. 'We stand before the Lord', says the Prayer.

For Origen (who adds outstretched hands and raised eyes), 'it's because one then carries in the body too, as it were, the image ('icon') of that special condition which befits the soul during prayer'.[5] Prayer is a spiritual uprightness, in other words. For St Irenaeus, it's 'a symbol of the resurrection'.[6] For St Basil, 'an image of the world to come'.[7] Yes, when at Easter the Lord rose, he 'came and *stood* among them' (Jn 20.19, 26; cf. Lk 24.36).

It would do us no harm to be more thoughtful even on this specific thing, even on how we carry ourselves in church, in choir. Ultimately, though, it's part of something larger. What the liturgy offers is a precious formation; or better perhaps, initiation. And it's an initiation into something that extends beyond liturgy in the strict sense, and out into the whole of our prayer and the whole of our life. It is initiation into the true Christian spirit, as St Pius X called it, and therefore into the meaning of a Christian body. And if I go with it, then, in some small way my poor, mortal flesh may become a body and give off in our poor world just a little of the glory of the risen One. No mean thing, if we think of it.

Notes

1. Huerre, 'Letter on Monastic Asceticism', from *Letters to my Brothers and Sisters* (Liturgical Press, Princeton, NJ, 1994).
2. Francis Thompson, 'Daisy', from *Works*, Vol. 1 (Burns & Oates Ltd, London, 1913) p. 3.
3. G. M. Hopkins, 'As kingfishers catch fire, dragonflies draw flame', from *Poems* (OUP, Oxford, 1967) p. 90.
4. St John Chrysostom, *Commentary on Romans*.
5. Origen, *On Prayer* 31, 2.
6. St Iranaeus, Fragment 7 of a *Treatise on Easter*.
7. St Basil, *Treatise on the Holy Spirit* 27.

9

Journeying Towards Easter I

It is a truism to say that Lent is a 'journey'. It is a journey of preparation for all those en route to baptism and/or reception into the Church, and a journey of purification for all the faithful. But when we leave on a journey we must know where we are going; and so with Lent. 'Let them look forward with the joy of spiritual longing to the holy feast of Easter', says St Benedict (*Rule* 49.7). Lent is a spiritual journey and its destination is Easter. So, first, we must try to understand the link between Lent and Easter or, more precisely, the real content of Easter. Then we can begin to appreciate Lent.

At one level, of course, Easter is just one more feast among others, and as such I might be unable to take part in the actual liturgies that make it up. I might be unwell. At another level, Easter is not just one feast among others, just as the Eucharist is not simply one sacrament among others. The Eucharist, because it contains Christ himself, is the sacrament of sacraments, and Easter, because of what it contains, is the feast of feasts. In the last resort, we're talking about the reality of Easter: not the celebrations per se, but what they celebrate, what they mediate. And what is that? 'He is the true Lamb who has taken away the sins of the world; who by dying has destroyed our death and by rising has restored our life.' It is hard to improve on those last two phrases of the first Easter preface. What we celebrate at Easter is the death and Resurrection of Christ, not as something private to him, but as entailing the death of everything deadly in us, and the irruption in us of a new and indestructible life. It is impossible, for someone in basically physical and emotional good health, to take part in, say, the Easter Vigil, the Easter Mass, Easter Vespers of the Roman rite – when celebrated in their fullness – without experiencing, feeling, tasting something of the wonder and depth of all this. The same holds, even more so many would say, in Easter celebrations of the Byzantine-rite Churches. 'Anyone who has, be it only once, taken part in that night which is "brighter than the day", who has tasted of that unique joy knows [that Easter is much more than one of the feasts, more than a yearly commemoration of a past event].'[1]

'This is the night, in which, having smashed the chains of death, Christ ascended as conqueror from the underworld' (*Exsultet*).

The preaching of the Apostles never separates the death of Christ from the Resurrection of Christ, and it never separates these events in themselves from what they are for and in ourselves. Likewise the liturgy. At the same time, it's safe to say that the emphasis of the Apostles fell especially on proclamation of the Resurrection. And so with the liturgy. So we can say that the reality of Easter is the Resurrection of Jesus Christ from the dead; is all contained and concentrated in that wonder of wonders.

There is nothing so final as a dead body. But there is one man who has been a dead body, dead for thirty-six hours, and is now a living body completely and eternally beyond the reach of death. This cannot be proved as I can prove, say, someone's age, or the fact that my father is dead. But it is, considering all the evidence, at least not unreasonable to accept the testimony of the original eyewitnesses; indeed, arguably unreasonable not to accept that testimony. But – to say it again – it is not the mere 'fact' that is the point. It might after all be no more than a one-off, or a personal compliment from some Superior Power to Jesus' integrity. Rather, 'dying he destroyed *our* death, rising he restored *our* life'. The new life, which almost two thousand years ago, broke out of a grave, has been given to us, to all who believe in Christ. And it was given to each of us initially when we were baptized, when, as St Paul says, 'we were buried with him into death

so that, as Christ was raised from the dead by the glory of the
Father, we too might walk in newness of life' (Rom 6.4). It
will be given to us fully, body, soul and spirit, when we have
shared fully in Christ's death and rise, at the end of time, in
glory.

At Easter then – journey's end – we celebrate Christ's
Resurrection as something that happened and still happens to
us. Each of us has received the gift of this new, indestructible,
ultimately divine life, and the power to accept it and live by
it. It is a gift which profoundly alters our attitude towards
everything in the world, including not least death. Death is
dead. When Christ is called the victor, the conqueror, it is in
the face of death as conqueror. But now the conqueror, the
last enemy, the one who always seemed to have the last word,
is conquered. Certainly, we still die. But it is now our faith
that, by dying and rising, Christ has changed the nature of
death. He has overcome death from inside, so to speak. He
has made it a 'passage', a passover, a *transitus*, into the
Kingdom of God, where death has no more dominion. The
tragedy of tragedies has become the ultimate victory. For St
Athanasius, this objective transformation is registered in the
psychology of Christians when they show themselves fearless
in the face of death, or at least overcome their fear of death.
He is thinking of the martyrs. 'Dying he destroyed our death,
rising he restored our life.' Out of the subterranean cavern of
Christ's empty tomb, there streams a quite new river of life.
And we have been plunged into it. That is Easter. The risen
Christ rises in us, in me. And every Christian, from the most
newly-baptized to the most mystically transfigured, can say
with St Paul, 'It is no longer I who live, but Christ who lives
in me' and 'he who is united to the Lord becomes one spirit
with him' (Gal 2.20; 1 Cor 6.17). This is the holy Easter we
look forward to with the joy of spiritual longing.

So far, so good. How often, though, we lose and betray
the new life of the risen Christ that has been given us. We
are weak and we find it hard to live constantly by faith, hope
and love on the level to which Christ has raised us. We
forget, we fail, we sin and our life becomes old again. The
new within us has the destiny of righting and raising the old

within us. Often though, even if not fatally, the old manages
to corrupt and depress the new. We do pray, for example,
and we have a living sense of God, a memory of God in us,
and every morning that may be re-stoked, but then when we
deal with each other we find ourselves functioning on the
purely natural plane. It probably is in the realm of human
relationships that the new life has its roughest time. Or again,
we spend so much energy simply protecting ourselves: justi-
fying ourselves, defending our interests, making sure we're
out of the reach of certain demands. The litany is endless,
boring and depressing. No need, then, to rehearse it. All
these things, little or great, simply mean that the old life still
holds sway, that the river of life isn't irrigating all my fields,
that life for me is somewhere other than the risen Christ. We
look for a life in what's only a tributary, not the river itself,
and often enough not even a decent tributary but some grubby
little ditch draining into it.

Enter, then, Lent. Enter Lent to help us repent and return
to the Easter life. It's a boat moored by our little stream to
help ferry us back to the great River. It's a refresher course,
recyclage. It helps us in all sorts of ways: simply by being
there, the forty days of it, a six-week statement of the glory
of Easter. If Easter requires such a preparation, Easter must
have something. A mountain taking forty days to climb cannot
be a molehill. It helps us by its active presence: its atmos-
phere, climate and the state of soul that it quietly communi-
cates, what the Byzantines call its 'bright sadness'. This
affects us imperceptibly, shapes our outlook and expectations,
our whole attitude to life. But always we must live Lent and
experience Lent against the horizon of the Resurrection, as a
return to, and a fresh release of risen life in us and around us.

Think of the asceticism of Lent, for example. Why fast, pray
and give alms? Simply and solely to regain the vision and the
taste of the Kingdom of God. We 'fast'; that is to say, we pull
ourselves back a little from some of the ordinary sustaining
pleasures of life, eating and drinking, sleeping and chatting,
novels and newspapers, perhaps because these do all tend to
become our life, to take up more space than that which reason
would allot them; because they tend to dull our spiritual senses,

our vision and taste of Christ and his gifts. We 'pray', that is to say, we raise our hearts and minds to God more often; we try to be more committed to sacred reading, precisely so that the vision and taste will be revived. We will be able to think and to see a little more like Christians, contemplatively, with the eyes of God. And we 'give alms', that is to say, we try to be a little more mindful of and attentive to our neighbours as precisely *the* sign of a revived Christ-life within us. It is an overflowing from the River of Life through us to others. In practice, it often just means being more faithful to our jobs.

This is Lent lived in the light of Easter. 'Dying he destroyed our death, rising he restored our life.' Lent is a restoration to life. Lent is a journey back and forwards. In the Early Church, and again today, the, or at least a main, purpose of Lent was to prepare catechumens for the sacraments of initiation: for baptism, confirmation and first reception of the Eucharist at Easter itself. And for us Easter is our return every year to our baptism, and Lent our preparation for that return. It is clearing out the rubble and the rubbish in the well – all so that the clear God-given water can bubble up more powerfully. It's a journey back home, like all good journeys, with home one day proving to be heaven.

The English 'Lent' once meant Spring. And as Lent goes on, Spring will become almost daily more evident to us, even if there are bursts of cold and snow. This can all help us pray, and understand Lent aright. Nature is on its journey to summer. With regard to Lent, someone has written, let us note the time of year in which it occurs: not in autumn, amidst the fog and falling leaves; not in winter, when the earth is dead and frozen; but in spring, when the frosts are ending, the days are growing longer, and the whole countryside returns to life. In the words of the Triodion (the Byzantine liturgical book for Lent): 'The springtime of the Fast has dawned, the flower of repentance has begun to open. O brethren, let us cleanse ourselves from all impurity, and sing to the Giver of Light: Glory be to Thee, who alone lovest mankind.' The Lenten season of repentance is a time of gladness, not of despondency: the Fast is a spiritual springtime, repentance is an opening flower, and Christ is made known to us in Lent as 'Giver of Light'.

Note

1. Alexander Schmemann, *Great Lent* (St Vladimir's Seminary Press, New York, 2003), p. 11.

10

Journeying Towards Easter II: Transfiguration

Only grace can change us. The old theology always said that, and experience confirms it. And the new theology only adds that grace is not a thing, grace is the presence of a Person. Grace is the presence of Christ.

Christ spent forty days in the desert. This was his Lent, the primal Lent, the Lent that sanctifies ours. But then he went public, he made himself present: for three years. And wasn't that a Lent for the first disciples, for the Twelve especially? Lent is a preparation for Easter. Weren't the Twelve being prepared for Easter? Lent is a catechumenate, a novitiate for the Christian life. Weren't the Twelve the first catechumens, the first novices? Lent is a time of penance, for a transformation of our understanding, our judging, our deciding. Weren't the Twelve being constantly asked precisely that?

Only grace can change us, and grace is the presence of Christ. Our prayers in Lent ask often enough that Lent will bear fruit. Did the three-year Lent of the first disciples bear fruit? Through failure, yes. And why? Because of the presence of Christ, and for no other reason. The Twelve lived with Christ and he with them. Think of Peter. At one level, Christ failed as spiritual father, catechist, Lenten pedagogue, novice master. There was Judas: a catastrophe. But take Peter: the leading pupil in the world's first and best RCIA course.[1] He makes his first communion, and then denies everything, falls into mortal sin. So much for a fruitful Lent. But then, when the impossible news comes, he runs to the tomb. He runs to it, and by the end of that day is believing and loving inadmissibly. And why? What brought him back? What filled the gap of that Friday and Saturday? Christ's eyes, Flannery O'Connor would say, and more, the memory of the Presence, the unique fragrance, the knowing that the last three years had been spent in the company of a Person unlike any other, who could only be called the Son, the Son of God. He ran to the tomb. Christ didn't let his pupil go. The Lent bore fruit, even through failure.

Only grace can change us, and grace is the presence of Christ. And how is Christ present to his modern disciples? Principally, says the Council, through the symbols and signs, the words and sacraments, of the Liturgy. And how, then, is he preparing his people for Easter and for what Easter symbolizes, heaven? Through the liturgy of Lent. And when is the Lenten liturgy most Lenten? On its Sundays. How powerful they are, these six Sundays of Lent. Only the Sundays of Eastertime, I think, approach them in power. They sum up, in six significant moments, the whole public ministry of Jesus, the whole 'apostolic Lent': his temptation in the desert, his transfiguration, the meeting with the Samaritan woman, the healing of the man born blind, the raising of Lazarus, the messianic entry into Jerusalem. They are like six great stones of a giant's causeway to the Triduum, to the Cross and the empty tomb and Easter morning. They are among the wonders of the Roman liturgy. And the centre of each of them is the Gospel of the day.

It is through these Sundays that the Church prepares for Easter. It's through them that Christ is present to us, sacramentally, and is preparing us, as he prepared the Twelve, for the paschal mystery and the life of the world to come.

The Sunday of the Transfiguration, traditionally the Second Sunday of Lent, has a history as the Church of Rome's original celebration of the Transfiguration. For over a thousand years the Church of Rome knew no other – until 1457, to be precise, when it accepted the feast of 6 August. If we go back to the time of St Leo, what we find is this: the Christians of Rome, fasting, would gather on Saturday evening at the church of St Mary in Transpontina, not far from St Peter's, and then process to St Peter's itself. There they would keep an all-night vigil. 'The faithful,' says Schuster,

> spent the whole of this night in prayer, singing psalms, and listen-
> ing to the reading, both in Greek and in Latin, of twelve lessons
> from Holy Scripture. The ceremony was enlivened by the beauti-
> ful melodies of the schola, by the brilliant light from the silver
> lamps . . . and by the perfume of incense and Eastern aromatics,
> with which the tomb of St Peter was incensed at the reading of
> each lesson.[1]

And the Gospel was the Gospel of the Transfiguration according to Matthew.

The climax was the ordaining of deacons and priests, and
then the celebrating of the Eucharist, the Bishop of Rome
presiding. By which time Sunday would be dawning. And that
was it: no other Mass that Sunday. We have one homily from
St Leo on the Transfiguration, preached at this all-night vigil,
in the year 445. The reason the vigil was held at St Peter's,
and not in another Roman church, was the ordinations. It was
thought appropriate that priestly power be transmitted in the
church where St Peter, the source, under Christ, of such
power, was buried. And St Peter's again was the reason for
the Gospel. It had to be a Gospel connected with the titular
saint of the Church, and Peter, certainly, features in the
Gospel of the Transfiguration. But he features in others too.
So why this one? It's hard to be certain. But Moses and Elijah
feature too: the two original practitioners of a forty-day fast.
Accidental reasons for what was surely an inspired choice.

With time, the all-night vigil passed away. It was the
custom in Rome only, not outside it. And as the Roman books
spread, it became necessary to create separate liturgies for the
Saturday and the Sunday. But the Transfiguration remained
the Gospel, until 1969, on both days. And now the new liturgy
has done everything to highlight this Second Sunday as the
Sunday of the Transfiguration.

As much as possible, the transfigured Christ is set before
us. At Mass, in the Gospel naturally; at the Introit: 'I seek
your face, O Lord; hide not your face from me'; in the
Collect; possibly in the Prayer over the Gifts when it talks of
offering sanctifying bodies as well as minds; certainly in the

Preface; again in the Communion antiphon; and finally in the post-communion Prayer, which refers to the 'glorious' mysteries we have just received (full of the glory of Christ, that is) and their effect of making us earth-dwellers already 'sharers of heavenly things', giving us a share in the Transfiguration, therefore.

'Jesus took with him Peter and James and John and led them up a high apart by themselves' (Mk 9:2). He led them up, and he leads us up also. He had just begun to teach them, 'plainly', says St Mark (8.32), 'that the Son of Man must suffer many things, and be rejected by the elders and the chief priests and the scribes, and be killed, and after three days rise again' (8.31). Peter would have none of this, nor would any of the others have understood. He took them up the mountain precisely because He wanted to take them up to Jerusalem, to the paschal mystery. And 'there in their presence he was transfigured', confirming Peter's confession of Him as the Christ, even (in Matthew) the Son of the Living God. 'His clothes became dazzlingly white, whiter than any earthly bleacher could make them' – bright with a heavenly brightness, therefore; proof that heaven was where He already belonged; augury of his exaltation, his return to heaven, and of his return from heaven; sign of his power to 'change our lowly body to be like his glorious body' (Phil 3.21). 'Elijah appeared to them with Moses; and they were talking with Jesus.' Both had seen the glory of God on the Mountain. But both the Law and the Prophets had foretold the Messiah's sufferings, and so they talked, as Luke famously has it, of his exodus 'which he was to accomplish at Jerusalem' (9.31). 'It is wonderful for us to be here,' says Peter, 'so let us make three tents.' He repeats his mistake. He has only half-heard. He 'thought that the time for the kingdom of God had already come,' says St Cyril, forgetting that it was not 'in this present time that the hopes of the saints would be fulfilled.' 'We must ask for patience before we ask for glory,' says St Leo, 'because the happiness of reigning can only come after the seasons of suffering' (*Sermo* 38.5).

Then the climax: the cloud comes, and 'a voice from the cloud, "This is my Son, the Beloved. Listen to him."' This means the glory is natural, the Resurrection inevitable. But also that the passion is the Father's will; that the Son has come to be a servant, to offer his life freely as a ransom for many. Only in the unity of Christ's Sonship can the baffling duality of passion and glory hold together. 'Listen to him,' says the Father. We know from the Gospel of John that the Son is the one who listens to the Father, and therefore speaks the words of God. 'Listen to him,' says the Father, even when he says that he must suffer, be rejected, be killed. 'Listen to him', even when he says: 'If any man would come after me, let him deny himself and take up his cross and follow me' (Mk 8.34); that you must lose your life as well. The Transfiguration gives us a foretaste or a foreglimpse of the Kingdom. Surely the last verse of the Gospel is heavy with irony: 'among themselves they discussed what "rising from the dead" could mean.' But at the same time it reminds us that it is 'through many tribulations we must enter the kingdom of God' (Acts 14.22), that we must ask for patience before we ask for glory. And that all this only makes sense, only coheres in sonship, surrender to the Father: Christ's sonship and our sonship.

Christ takes us to Easter as he took his first disciples, by way of his transfiguration. He wants us to know that glory is certain, that the Father cannot possibly abandon his Beloved. He wants us to know that there is only one path to glory: through the passion, and that this passion can be made an action, a giving of self to the Father for others. He wants us to become what we became at baptism, what he is from all eternity: a son of God. 'This is my Son, the Beloved; listen to him.' That is certainly the line. It 'must always echo in our ears,' says St Leo (*Sermo* 38.8). And perhaps its most important word is not 'Son', not 'listen', but 'beloved'. A son has nothing of his own; that's the experience of suffering. A son has everything the Father has: that's the glorification. But whether dying or rising, needing patience or being given glory, a son is always the beloved.

Did Peter learn his lesson? Did he listen? Well, yes, he ran to the tomb. But that's not the only proof. Another proof is his own tomb, on the hill of the Vatican. He laid down his life for the sake of Christ and of the Gospel. And it's worth remembering that the liturgy of the Transfiguration springs from that: from his Church, his tomb, his obedience.

Note

1. RCIA, 'The Rite of Christian Initiation of Adults', is the course followed by those wishing to become members of the Catholic Church.

11

Palm Sunday

Now before the festival of the Passover, Jesus knew that his hour had come to depart from this world and go to the Father.

(Jn 13.1)

'Going', 'going away', 'going to the Father'. In the Gospel of John, that is the meaning of Jesus' death and Resurrection and Ascension. 'I come from the Father and have come into the world; again, I am leaving the world and am going to the Father' (Jn 16.28). And the disciples exclaim in response, 'Yes, now you are speaking plainly, not in any figure of speech.' There could hardly be a plainer idea than that of 'going', moving to a destination.

And it is, of course, a word from Exodus: 'Moses and Aaron went to Pharaoh and said, "Thus says the Lord, the God of Israel, 'Let my people go, that they may hold a feast to me in the wilderness.'" But Pharaoh said, "Who is the Lord, that I should heed his voice and let Israel go? I do not know the Lord moreover and I will not let Israel go."' Seven chapters later the mighty Pharaoh has been broken: 'He summoned Moses and Aaron in the night, and said, "Rise up, go forth from among my people, both you and the people of Israel; and go, serve the Lord, as you said. Take your flocks and herds, as you have said, and be gone; and bless me also!"' (Ex 5.1–2; 12.31–32). God Himself 'goes out' (11.4), 'goes before' (32.1), 'goes with' (34.9) the people, and the people follow, Israel the first-born son (4.22–23). He goes and meets his Father at the foot of the mountain where the covenant is made, and eventually, at journey's end, in the Temple. All this anticipates the exodus, the Passover of Jesus. And the Passover of Jesus enables us, too, to go, to go to the Father.

I think this is the simplest, truest key to Holy Week and Easter. And Easter really should blow us apart on this point, make us long to proclaim the message to the end of the earth. Life has a purpose. Life is a journey. Life is going to the Father.

It was once pointed out to me that English is the only European language that uses the phrases 'pass on', 'pass away' of dying. A remarkable testimony to our Christian inheritance! Living and dying are a passing – from this world to the Father.

What are we doing, then, when we celebrate Easter? We are keeping open in our hearts the going to the Father which Christ has given back to the human race. We are keeping it open in this time – against every attempt of the mystery of iniquity to close it up again. We are saying what we say every Thursday at Vespers: 'Search me, God, and know my heart! Try me, and know my thoughts! And see if there be any wickedness in me, and lead me in the way everlasting' (Ps 138.23–24).

So much comes to mind round this.

A highway shall be there, and it shall called the Holy Way; the unclean shall not pass over it, and fools shall not err therein. No lion shall be there, nor shall any ravenous beast come up on it; they shall not be found there, but the redeemed shall walk there.
(Is 35.8–9)

Redemption means having a way, the true way, a way to the Father. Any human being can find a way in his work and in his relationships. Those are the two staples in most people's lives. But how hard it is for many to experience that really as a way. Work, if you can get it, can be soul-destroying, and relationships can go horribly wrong. So many lives are so empty: for lack of anything to live for, for anywhere to go.

And neither work nor human relationships – though they are real, if secondary, 'ends', though they do very much mobilize us – can be our focal end or activate us at the deepest level. 'Coming from God, going toward God, man lives a fully human life only if he freely lives by his bond with God' (*Catechism of the Catholic Church* 44). God has to shine upon us and open up the path. Then we can acknowledge the Father to whom we can go. Think of the Prodigal Son: 'I will arise and go to my Father' (Lk 15.18). Not just empty words, it's much more; it's a memory. 'Send out your light and your truth; let them lead me, let them bring me to your holy hill and to your dwelling' (Ps 42.3).

In the monk's way to the Father I think that there are three especially difficult and delicate periods. The first comes at the beginning of the monastic life, when he has to unlearn the ways of the world and learn the ways of God and of community life. The second can come in the middle – the famous mid-life crisis of the 'roaring forties' – when the motives that sustained him hitherto no longer have the same appeal, and his whole outlook changes. The third comes not at the end, but at the end of a monk's active, public life; when, in secular parlance, he comes to the age of retirement, when what filled so many years of his life is taken away. Similar periods occur in the secular life, in marriage, in the Christian life, and so on.

I do not intend to analyze these experiences here. I want solely to connect them with going to the Father, to set them in the perspective of faith. Indeed, nothing but grace can, not just get one through them, but turn them into positive experiences which make one more completely belonging to God. And that is the point: by grace, they become part of our going to the Father. By grace, they carry the stamp of the paschal mystery. They are a dying to something, a purification, and a rising to something better, an enlargement.

'Now, before the festival of the Passover, Jesus knew that his hour had come to depart from this world and go to the Father.' From the human point of view, what was coming was a rejection, an injustice, a tragedy. Yet, as for him, so for us; thanks to him, so for us: 'A highway shall be there'. Whether one is young or middle-aged or getting old, 'a highway shall be there' and 'the redeemed shall walk there'. 'God is faithful, and he will not let you be tempted beyond your strength, but with the temptation will also provide the way of escape, that you may be able to endure it' (1 Cor 10.13).

Here is some wisdom from the son of Sirach:

> Do not give yourself over to sorrow, and do not afflict yourself deliberately. Gladness of heart is the life of man, and the rejoicing of a man is length of days. Delight your soul and comfort your heart, and remove sorrow far from you, for sorrow has destroyed many, and there is no profit in it. Jealousy and anger shorten life, and anxiety brings on old age too soon. A man of cheerful and good heart will give heed to the food he eats.
>
> (Sir 30.21–25)

God is the Creator of the seven ages of man, God is their Redeemer and God is their Sanctifier.

'A highway shall be there.' In a funeral homily for a French monk who died recently came these words: 'Celibacy took him years to conquer.' Various couples supported him, women respectfully helped him. He once wrote: 'The lack of a wife and children has sometimes been crucifying. How many times I would say to God in tears: "My God, it's You! Keep me for You! It is You who chose me."' And elsewhere:

> For six years I experienced a terrifying loneliness. One day I spoke about it to a friend. She said to me, 'Loneliness is unavoidable, even in a married life. One has to pass through it.' That came to me as God's answer. When I accepted it, I was no longer alone and I was able to keep my heart free. Now, I'm seventy. And I feel like a child lost in wonder at what has happened within me.

'A highway shall be there', a way to the Father. This is the meaning of Easter.

There is this beautiful passage in Hebrews:

> Therefore, brethren, since we have confidence to enter the sanctuary by the blood of Jesus, by the new and living way which he opened for us through the curtain, that is, through his flesh, and

since we have a great high priest over the house of God, let us draw near with a true heart in full assurance of faith, with our hearts sprinkled clean from an evil conscience and our bodies washed with pure water. (10.19–22)

There is a 'new living way' into the sanctuary, into the presence of God, and that 'way' is Jesus' flesh, according to the more probable interpretation: his crucified and glorified flesh. That is the Book of Hebrews' way of saying what John says in the first words of chapter 13.

At Easter, I remember the stories of Pannonhalma, the great Benedictine monastery in Hungary founded one thousand years ago. Under the Communists, Catholic schools were closed and Catholic catechesis forbidden. But the liturgy could go on, and the young Catholics of Hungary could come to Pannonhalma for Holy Week and Easter. And that was enough. It sustained the faith. It begot, too, at least one saint, Monika Tamar, who helped in the clandestine refounding of Cistercian life for women and died at twenty-five. Her diary has been translated into German and French at least. She wrote:

This Easter feast was the first that permitted me to experience what I have accepted with my understanding for a very long time: this life is only a brief passage of transition that flies away quickly. The only truth is the risen Lord. It is still painful to be far away from him, and how much do I feel this on this day! But I can never again forget this unique experience, which lasted only a few minutes. It is not this life that is reality for me: the other life, beyond the grave, is a thousand times more real [translated from the French by Dom Hugh].

That passage echoes, as she says, a 'unique experience': a grace clearly appropriate to a young person predestined to die young. Would any of us say heaven is a thousand times more real than this life? But surely we can take from her that life is 'passage' and 'transition' and that 'the only truth is the risen Lord'. And it was Easter, it was the liturgical celebration of a monastic community, that brought that home, or that the Lord used to bring it home.

I've said before: the greatest public service a monastery can perform is the full, dignified, fervent and prayerful celebration of the Easter mysteries. This is true at the 'mystical' level, invisibly, in the communion of saints. This is true at the 'political' level, visibly, for us actually celebrating the feast. If for one soul anywhere or for one of us or for one of our fellow-worshippers Easter means the re-opening of a 'way' to the Father, the end of a blockage, a return of hope, and the impinging of the reality of the risen Christ, then the celebration has been worth it. And, of course, it always does mean that, at some level, because the liturgy conveys the grace it symbolizes, including the grace to receive the grace.

Here it is a great temptation to evoke St Benedict's *transitus*, his passing – St Gregory describes the scene so beautifully. We recall it every evening. It's an icon not just of an ideal monastic death, but of monastic life. And, since Benedict is an abbot, a father, it's an icon of the life of a monastery. He dies standing in the oratory (the place of psalmody and prayer) with his hands raised to heaven (in the attitude of Moses and of Christ on the Cross: triumphant intercession, unflagging praise) and actually praying. This is the picture, if you like, of paschal man, of man following Christ in his return to the Father, of man ascending. And that is the picture every monk should have in his heart, and every monastery. A monastery is a visible sign of the mystery of the Ascension, drawing everything upward: 'his soul was seen to ascend heavenwards'. God the Father loves monasteries, monks and nuns, because he sees the mystery of the Son's Ascension being completed in them. He sees humanity and human culture returning to him in them. And as the ascending Son blessed the disciples he was leaving, so the Father will bless us and lift us up too. But he 'passed over', St Benedict, 'strengthened by holy communion' and 'supporting his failing limbs in the arms of his disciples'. To live a life of going to the Father, of having turned to the Father, to maintain that picture, is, of course, beyond our powers. But not if we are eating the glorified body and allow ourselves, in our weaknesses of body and character, to be kept upright by our brethren.

So we're beginning Holy Week. Tempers always fray a bit

at this time of year, and in a sense they're meant to. But let's be patient and well disposed towards each other. A curious fact in the spiritual life, at least of some: the harder we're trying ourselves, the more we tend to become critical of others. I give up cheese but not tut-tutting. In fact, the less cheese, the more tut-tutting. 'O my dear Wormwood: it's such a delicious sight! An unmortified irascible appetite betraying an unmortified concupiscible. The sort of thing that makes demonic life worth living!' Mutual denigration is a poison, acid rain. 'May God, our God, bless us' and we bless each other, especially when we're all trying to bless God together.

So we enter Holy Week. Today we commemorated the entry into Jerusalem; tomorrow, it's the anointing at Bethany, on Tuesday and Wednesday, the foresight of Judas' betrayal and Peter's denial. On Thursday, Lent ends and the Triduum opens. The fast of Good Friday is not the remedial fasting of Lent but a paschal fast, a fast 'because the Bridegroom has been taken away'. With the Easter Vigil, the Easter season opens, as much a season as Lent. And as Lent looks to the Triduum, so the Easter season looks to the Ascension and Pentecost, when the going to the Father is completed. 'The Passion of Christ,' says St Thomas, 'promoted and lifted up. It did not oppress.' Why? Because ' "he was passing from this world to the Father", that is making human nature a sharer in the glory of the Father.'[1]

Let us take the mother of Jesus as our companion. She was there, following through her faith and her motherly feeling. She stood, says St John. She was silent. She believed, was silent, suffered with. And the events – from the Passion through to Pentecost – had their effect, bore their fruit in her, promoting and lifting up as St Thomas says. She became the mother of all believers. She received the gift of intercession. At our levels, the same is offered us. With Mary, then, may we, in St Augustine's words, pass over with the passover of Christ, lest we pass away with this passing world.

Note

1. Aquinas, *In Joannem*.

12

Blood and Water

Good Friday Homily 2004

One of the soldiers pierced his side with a lance and immediately there came out blood and water.

(Jn 19.34)

We are in Good Friday and this liturgy unlike any other. The images are veiled, the altar stripped. The celebrant prostrates. Isaiah holds up the image of the suffering Servant, the Letter to the Hebrews the compassionate High Priest; St John leads out his regal Lamb of God. Christ comes before us in shadow and light. In a moment, the ten intercessions follow, the Church's arms stretching out as far as Christ's. The Cross is unveiled to a rising chant, and we give our kisses against the counterpoint of the Reproaches: 'My people, what have I done to you?' The 'dry Mass' follows, the simple communion. And we go.

Immediately there came out blood and water.

This is 'the Passion of the Christ' according to the liturgy. Not simplistic, not a Passion play, not an orgy of violence. It is something of its own. And it stretches us two ways at once, like the crucified Hands. Good Friday has something appalling about it, something that throws to the ground, and Good Friday has something that comforts like nothing else and sends us home blessed. Good Friday is a catastrophe. Good Friday is grace.

One of the soldiers pierced his side with a lance.

A catastrophe. The catastrophe. 'He came to his own, and his own received him not' (Jn 1.11). Every other catastrophe is a catastrophe because it partakes of this one. It's as if, in the Passion of Christ, sin and Satan, our hostility to Love and hatred one of another, our dark, all-devouring self-centredness, at last find the object they've been longing for: the Lamb of God, unqualified Goodness, Truth and Love in the flesh. Able to be seized and bound, ridiculed and misjudged, beaten up and crucified. It's the great anti-liturgy, anti-feast of history, and every other nastiness, from grand-scale genocides to our own domestic squalors, is simply Sin doing whatever 'in memory of' this. An anti-Eucharist. Or to change the image, it's as if, in Jerusalem, that day, the human No – from Christian, Jew and Gentile, all of us – found its voice. And every other 'no', great or small, every 'no' to God and truth and one another's good, is simply echo, miserable mimicry of what was said and done, that day, to the Word made flesh.

'And immediately there came out blood and water.' Immediately. It was already there. It was waiting. Whose initiative was the Passion? It seems like Judas' or the Sanhedrin's or Pilate's; in other words, ours. It was not. The Passion comes from God's mercy. It comes from the free self-offering of Christ, his willingness to be the Lamb, his readiness to take God's judgement on sin onto himself. The Passion and Death are Love's initiative, Love older than the hills, and older and younger than Sin. And once Sin had danced its *danse macabre* on the place called the place of the skull; once it had done its worst and made its final lunge, 'immediately there came out blood and water'. Immediately this something other and greater than Sin was revealed: the Grace behind, beneath, beyond. The catastrophe was turned around; and behind the hubbub, in their Cross-broken hearts, the mother of Jesus, the other Marys, and the disciple Jesus loved – we the Church! – caught that quiet Yes infinitely more resonant than the No.

'Immediately there came out blood and water.' Out of the blood of this sacrifice came the water of life. The spring of paradise (Gen 2.6, 10) re-opened, Isaiah's water in the desert

(35.6). The river Ezekiel had foreseen pouring out of the Temple, making even the Dead Sea fresh (47.1). Zechariah's fountain in Jerusalem (12.10; 13.1). In other words, the Spirit Jesus had promised would flow from his heart (Jn 7.37). *Te fons salutis, Trinitas!* The Father has loved his Son, for us, all the way to the Cross, and the Son has loved him in return, for us. And out of that love to the end, that love to the giving of blood, comes the Spirit – for us, into us. For the cleansing of 'sin and impurity' (Zech 13.1). For conversion and forgiveness. For life and hope and new beginnings. For secret sustenance when catastrophes come, and the Passion play is re-enacted. For quenching the thirst of the heart and giving rebirth to the world.

Immediately there came out blood and water. The Love and the Life older and younger, greater and deeper; comfort and joy. Coming on us as well, successors to that small group beneath the Cross. We have stumbled on the hidden stream, discovered the secret. And we must give witness and comfort in turn: out of this death, out of God's heart, Father and Son, comes the Holy Spirit! So, saved by this death, consoled by this gift, let us stand now and pray to the Father for everyone.

13

The Paschal Mystery

The phrase 'the paschal mystery' may occasionally fall on our ears or meet our eyes: in some of the prayers of Lent and Eastertide, in the odd homily perhaps, in writings on the liturgy, in worthy compendiums of the Church's faith like the *Catechism of the Catholic Church*. We may be aware it has to do with the death and Resurrection of Christ, and so with Easter, but it remains, I suspect, a little alien and slightly baffling. And this is a shame, for it is a phrase which takes us to the heart of our faith and, as it does so, draws together many things we tend to separate, and so can help give us the sense of at last understanding, at last finding the centre, and therefore finding life.

'Understand, therefore, beloved, how it is new and old, eternal and temporary, perishable and imperishable, mortal and immortal, this mystery of the Pasch.' What Melito, a second-century bishop of Sardis, in the earliest known use of the phrase, here says about the *reality of* the paschal mystery – 'it is new and old' at once – can be said about the *phrase* too. In its Latin form, *sacramentum paschale*, it is found in the ancient Roman liturgical books, but it was a French Protestant minister turned Catholic and priest, Louis Bouyer, who, in 1945 (building on the pioneering work of the German Benedictine, Dom Odo Casel), made it the title of an epoch-making study of the liturgy of the last days of Holy Week, *Le Mystère Pascal*, and so began the process of making the 'old' 'new' again. Could one say the rediscovery of 'paschal mystery' springs from Europe's experience of death and resurrection in and after the Second World War? In any case, Vatican II took up the phrase, especially in its Constitution on the Sacred Liturgy; so have the post-conciliar liturgical books; so has John Paul II; so, as mentioned above, has the *Catechism of the Catholic Church*; and so have many liturgists, theologians and Christian thinkers. When Hans Urs von Balthasar's great study of the death and Resurrection of Christ was translated into English, it was given the simple Latin title *Mysterium Paschale*. It is worth us all taking up this phrase! It combines two separate phrases of St Paul: 'For *Christ our Passover* [i.e. passover Lamb] has been sacrificed' (1 Cor 5:7), and 'the *mystery of Christ*' (Eph 3.4; Col 4.3), and by so doing focuses the whole theological content of the latter – the whole 'revelation of the mystery' (Rom 16.25) – in the Passover or Pasch.

Let us explore a little further.

John the Evangelist begins the second part of his Gospel, devoted to the passion and Resurrection of Jesus, with the words: 'Now before the feast of the Passover, when Jesus knew that his hour had come to depart out of this world to the Father, having loved his own who were in the world, he loved them to the end' (Jn 13:1). When we speak of the paschal mystery, we are speaking, *at the level of history*, about Jesus' passing from 'this world to the Father', a passing that coincided, in Jerusalem *c*.AD30 with the annual Jewish celebration of the Passover. We refer to everything that comprised Jesus' passing/passover: his death and Resurrection most centrally, but also what immediately prepared for them: the Last Supper with the disciples, the Agony (i.e. Struggle) in the Garden and the rest of the Passion, and what immediately followed them, his Ascension, his 'Session' at the right hand of the Father and too, as the consummation of all this, the sending of the Holy Spirit on the first believers at Pentecost. We refer, therefore, to the climax of Jesus' life, to the events which, in the Christian view, not only formed the *raison d'être* of that life and of the Incarnation itself, but are also the source of human salvation, the turning-point of history, and the decisive manifestation of God's love for humanity.

At *the level of liturgy*, we are referring, it's immediately clear, to what is recalled annually at Holy Week and Easter, weekly every Sunday, and even daily in the Eucharist: 'Christ's death, his descent among the dead, his resurrection and his ascension to your right hand' (Eucharistic Prayer IV), that is, to the transcendentally salvific presence and effectiveness of these historical events. We are referring, in fact, to what is under differing aspects the content of every sacramental and liturgical celebration. 'In the liturgy of the Church', says the *Compendium* of the *Catechism* (n. 222), 'it is his own paschal mystery that Christ signifies and makes present.' At the level of Christian living, we are referring to the pattern of our own redemption: as St Paul writes, 'we were buried, therefore, with him by baptism into death, so that as Christ was raised from the dead by the glory of the Father, we too might walk in newness of life. For if we have been united with him in a death like his, we shall certainly be united with him in a resurrection like his' (Rom 6.4–5). The perspectives open up, one after the other.

The Greek translation of the Hebrew word for the Passover (*pesach*) was *Pascha*. This became in turn a word for the Christian Easter, in Latin also; hence *Pasqua* in Italian, *Pâques* in French. (It is ill-advised, incidentally, to translate the Latin liturgical phrases *mysterium/sacramentum paschale* simply as 'Easter mystery'; in that case, the Old Testament reference, which is integral, disappears).

We call this a *mystery* because, it is at root, an action of God in human history beyond our total comprehension, beyond the mastering power of our mind; because the whole sequence of events springs from the holiness, the transcendence of God, and leads us, beyond ourselves, to him; because it can only be accepted in faith and entered with the grace of the Holy Spirit. We call it the *paschal mystery*, because it is the fulfilment of the most decisive event in Israel's history, the Exodus, when God passed over (spared) the suffering Israelites in Egypt and they passed over the Red Sea, out of slavery into freedom. We call it the paschal mystery, because it contains the 'mystery', i.e. the true, hidden meaning, not only of that Exodus (the historical passover), but also of its ritual commemoration (the liturgical passover) and of the sacrificed Lamb (also called the passover) at its heart. We call it the paschal mystery because Christ's death and Resurrection was his passage from this world to the Father, the new Exodus, in which he opened up a way for us to pass with him, in liturgy and life, from the old creation to the new; because he is the true Lamb of God who takes away the sins of the world, whose flesh and blood we eat and drink, having crossed the Red Sea of baptism, in the freedom of the children of God.

Perhaps something of the value of this phrase is already clear. It has the power to bring many things together; it synthesizes. It can hold together, 'without confusion or separation', the story of Israel and its culmination in the story of Jesus, Old Testament and New, anticipation and fulfilment. It can hold together the painful and glorious aspects of Jesus' passover. It is often said that Western Christianity privileges the Passion of Christ, Eastern Christianity his Resurrection. One-sidedness is a possibility. Here neither is privileged at the expense of the other. There is a single movement involving distinct moments, something as there is when the Gospel of John speaks of Christ's being 'lifted up', with the *double entendre* of lifted up on the Cross and lifted up in the Ascension. And there is still scope for prayer to penetrate and mind to probe the mysterious relationships between the two sides of the single, complex mystery. There is a holding together, too, of liturgy and life. The Exodus and the Jewish Passover, the Passover and Jesus' passover to the Father, Jesus' passover and its re-presentation in Christian liturgy, its liturgical representation and its living out in a crucified and risen life: the phrase makes all these connections. Vatican II and the *Catechism* stress particularly the paschal mystery as the point of synthesis for the whole of Christian liturgy. Everything in Christian liturgy – from the celebration of the Eucharist, the memorial of the mystery in its wholeness, to the celebration of a saint, who has passed from life to death after the pattern of Christ; from Baptism which first immerses the believer in the death and Resurrection of Christ to the Liturgy of the Hours which prolongs in time the prayer of the crucified and ascended One; from Marriage which enables a man and woman to embody the marriage of Christ and the Church brought about on the Cross to monastic Profession which conforms the monk or nun to the crucified Christ in order to the sharing of his life in the Spirit – takes its meaning and reality from the paschal mystery and leads on, in noble and generous hearts, to its inscribing in human life.

Any of this, needless to say, could be expanded upon, and yet, even when it is, something still more important remains. It is not a question of a 'natty' phrase or even of a theological open sesame. It is, rather, like a finger pointing to the very heart and centre of Christ, Christianity and human existence. The Fathers of the Church will say that God became man so that, as man, he might die, and as God, rise: in other words, that the paschal mystery was the centre and goal of the incarnate Son's whole being and mission. 'I have a baptism with which I am to be baptized.' And what is true of him is true of man, of us. The paschal mystery has been set by God the Father at the heart of things. Even the patterns of nature and the innate rhythms of human life suggest it; dying and rising are everywhere. All the more does the Holy Spirit urge us, body, soul and spirit, towards it. The paschal mystery, simply, is truth and life. To refuse it leaves us with nothing; to consent to it is life in its fullness. 'His paschal mystery', says the *Catechism of the Catholic Church*,

is a real event that occurred in our history, but it is unique: all other historical events happen once, and then they pass away, swallowed up in the past. The paschal mystery of Christ, by contrast, cannot remain only in the past, because by his death he destroyed death, and all that Christ is – all that he did and suffered for all men – participates in the divine eternity, and so transcends all times while being made present in them all. The event of the Cross and Resurrection *abides* and draws everything toward life (1085).

'The Christian faith,' wrote Jean Daniélou in 1945,

has only one object: the mystery of Christ dead and risen. But this single mystery subsists under different modes: it is prefigured in the Old Testament, it is accomplished historically in the earthly life of Christ, it is contained in mystery in the sacraments, it is lived mystically in souls, it is accomplished socially in the Church, it is consummated eschatologically in the heavenly kingdom.[1]

Such is the expanse of what another second century homilist called 'the cosmic and universal mystery of the pasch'. Such is what our Easter is about.

Note
1. R. Taft, *The Liturgy of the Hours in East and West* (Liturgical Press, Collegeville, 1985), p. 371.

14

He is Risen!

Easter Vigil Homily 2005

After the sabbath, and towards dawn on the first day of the week, Mary of Magdala and the other Mary went to see the sepulchre.

Mt 28.1

Our Russian guides then took us to [his] air-raid shelter. I went down to the bottom and saw the room in which he and his mistress had committed suicide, and when we came up again they showed us the place where his body had been burned. We were given the best first-hand accounts available at the time of what had happened in these final scenes.

So wrote Winston Churchill of his visit, at the end of the Second World War, to the infamous bunker of Adolf Hitler in Berlin.

After the Sabbath . . .

Clear and strange the contrast. Strange how men who have stood on podiums haranguing crowds end cowering underground before the terrors they've released.

On Ash Wednesday we heard, 'Remember, man, that you are dust and unto dust you shall return.' And tonight two women make their way to another of the dead, entombed, returned to the ground, on his way to dust with good and bad alike. They go, a duo of grief, to 'see the sepulchre', Matthew says. They were going down, metaphorically at least, their hopes and the Man they loved crucified and buried. Which of us hasn't stood by gravesides looking down, feeling the gravity, the pull of the dust?

Just before the Easter week he died, George Mackay Brown, poet of Orkney, published 'The Harrowing of Hell', brief and exquisite.[1]

> He went down the first step.
> His lantern shone like the morning star.
> Down and round he went
> Clothed in his five wounds.

Six steps follow: on the second he meets Solomon, on the third David, on the fourth Joseph, on the fifth Jacob, on the sixth Abel.

> On the seventh step down
> The tall primal dust [Adam]
> Turned with a cry from digging and delving.

Fine line! 'Turned with a cry from digging and delving' hopelessly, fruitlessly down. 'Tomorrow,' ends the poem,

> the Son of Man will walk in a garden
> Through drifts of apple-blossom.

'And all at once there was a great earthquake', and the women, surely, turned with a cry. Mary Magdalene would again, we know. And their vision of the tomb becomes sight of an angel. And they hear the words: 'He is not here, he has risen, as he said. Come and see the place where he lay, go quickly and tell his disciples.' And the duo of grief, down among the dead, turns with a cry from digging and delving. Suddenly awestruck and joyful, they're running 'away from the tomb'.

Someone has been down before them and further: the One who didn't think equality with God something to be grasped, but humbled himself and became as all men are, dust for dust, and humbled himself still more to death on a cross, and went on down to the underworld – down and round the seven steps all the way to Adam. Then, at the cry of the Father, he turned and came up. And as he climbed he cried:

> I command you, Awake . . . Arise from the dead; I am the life of
> the dead. Arise, O man, work of my hands, arise you who were
> fashioned in my image. Rise, let us go hence, you in me and I in
> you'. (Ancient Holy Saturday Homily)

For 'tomorrow the Son of Man will walk in a garden/ Through
drifts of apple-blossom'.

The women, meanwhile, running, running, awestruck and
joyful, away from the tomb. 'And there, coming to meet
them, was Jesus. "Rejoice," he said. And the women came up
to him.' And suddenly, in a gesture, there's revealed the why
of it all, of the Fall, why the fault is *felix*, happy. The sight
of the tomb turns with a cry into sight of Him, and 'falling
down before Him, they clasped his feet'. Falling down, *prosk-
inesis*, adoration, dust before divinity, deep calling to deep,
new depths of love answering the unimagined depths of
God's. Now they know there is nothing Christ cannot do, no
dark, deep place he cannot raise from, nothing they cannot
hope for. Everything's come right.

They're the Church, these women: us. 'When we were
baptized in Christ Jesus we were baptized into his death' – as
thousands are being tonight, all over the world; in other
words, 'when we were baptized we went into the tomb with
him and joined him in death, so that as Christ was raised from
the dead by the Father's glory, we too might live a new life'
(Rom 6:3–4 JB). We, too, turning with a cry, like Adam,
from fruitless digging and delving. We, too, not going down
and round a tyrant's bunker, coming up to scattered ash, but
going down by faith into the life-giving Tomb, falling down
in worship at his feet, and rising, hearts enlarged, to run with
unspeakable sweetness of love in the way of his commands.
For 'tomorrow – it's already tomorrow – the Son of Man will
walk in a garden/ Through drifts of apple-blossom.' He has
risen from the dead and conquered everything.

Note

1. George Mackay Brown, 'The Harrowing of Hell', in *Northern Lights* (John Murray, London, 1999), p. 24, reproduced by kind permission of John Murray (Publishers) Ltd.

15

Resurrection

Easter the beautiful, Easter, the Easter of the Lord.
Easter full of overflowing majesty has risen and shines
for us. Easter! Let us embrace one another in joy!
Easter, deliverance from sorrow . . . Today holy Easter
is manifested to us, the new and holy Passover, the
mystical Passover, the all-honourable Passover, the
Passover which is Christ the Redeemer, the immaculate
Passover, the mighty Passover, the Passover of the faith-
ful, the Passover that opens the gates of paradise for us,
the Passover that gives light to all the faithful.

Byzantine Easter Matins

How do we do justice to the power and glory of the Resurrection? The more I think about that, the more it seems to me
that only two ways approach adequacy: first, the celebration
of the liturgy, and second, holiness of life. It is the Church in
her Easter liturgies that goes out to meet the Lord as he rises,
like the women going to the tomb to anoint him, and the
Church in her saints, her fully risen ones, who falls to the
ground and clasps his feet. But there is room too for those
who come limping along after: the theologians and the artists
(poets, musicians, painters) and our poor selves. Yes, we too,
we want to run to the tomb, see the Lord, and sing the hymns
of the Risen One. How could we not?

The Resurrection is the declaration of *Life,* the triumph of
life. A life that is stronger than death. We are all alive
already, of course, but with a life that so often seems at

loggerheads with itself and will inevitably be claimed by death, as has been the life of our forbears and of an ever lengthening list of those we have known. We are immortally alive in our souls, we may say, but then what kind of life would that entail beyond the grave? Nothing of itself but an unending prolongation of capacity. But with the Resurrection, Life, true and unending Life, a *blessed* immortality has dawned upon us. It is a life that comes from above, from the Father, divine life; it is the filial life of the Son of God now present in humanity; it is a life universal in its destination, its bearer the 'new Adam', the 'universal brother'; it is a life that cannot be overwhelmed by human evil as was shown on the Cross; it is a life that is stronger than death, being precisely the life of the *risen* Christ, the one who has died and has come to life. It is the presence and gift of the Holy Spirit. It is the life to receive which we were originally given life in the beginning, life with a small 'l' being ordered to it, *bios* to *zoé*, the psychic to the spiritual, the natural to the supernatural. It is a 'new life', which, as it comes into its inheritance, demands the death and works the transformation of the old. It is the life that fills the Church and makes her Christ's Body and Bride, our Mother and the beginning of a new humanity: the life of her ministered word and sacraments, the life of her loving, the life that keeps her buoyant on the ocean of time.

It is communicated to believers one by one by the Holy Spirit through the Church and is lived out by them, in this life, as faith, hope and charity. It revives the struggling sinner, inspires chastity, poverty and obedience, and flowers in the saints. It is present, too, beyond the Christian frontiers, and is offered as a real possibility to every human being. It is hidden from the eyes of the world and known only to faith, but because of it the world is kept in being, the sun rises, spring comes round and children are born. It is 'afflicted in every way, but not crushed, persecuted but not forsaken, struck down but not destroyed', weak but strong, always being given up to death, only to rise again (cf. 2 Cor 4.8f). It fills the souls of those who die in the Lord, giving them the vision of the Father and bonding the living and the dead into one. It will, finally, transform and transfigure our mortal bodies and the entirety of the cosmos. All this in and from the risen Christ. All this made known at Easter. Praise to You, Lord Jesus Christ!

We have celebrated, we are celebrating the *liturgy* of Easter. But how do we keep the Easter of *holiness,* the Easter of heart and life? Three ways suggest themselves.

Iam credite! 'Now believe!' (cf. Jn 20.27) Firstly, by believing. There is this indissoluble link between the Resurrection and faith. 'O foolish men, and slow of heart to believe' (Lk 24.25). The Resurrection, by its very nature, asks us the question, 'Do you believe?' Nothing else in the Christ story puts it so sharply. Then, in the Gospel stories of the empty tomb and appearances, we see this faith fighting its way to the surface through the inevitable doubts and hesitations. Think of Mary Magdalene, the disciples on the way to Emmaus, Thomas. It emerges as something both reasonable and above reason. Looking at the evidence as a whole, it is surely more reasonable to follow the first believers and accept the early Christian claim to have discovered the tomb empty and to have met a resurrected Jesus than to dismiss it as the product of a deliberate lie or wishful thinking or collective hallucination or the objectification of an inner sense of Jesus' enduring worth. And yet to accept the credibility of the Apostles' witness doesn't turn it into a matter of 2+2=4, doesn't abolish the need to take the small, great step from the judgement, 'This holds water, this is believable' to the affirmation, 'I believe'. 'No one,' says the *Catechism,*

> was an eyewitness to Christ's Resurrection and no evangelist describes it. Still less was its innermost essence, his passing over to another life, perceptible to the senses. Although the Resurrection was an historical event that could be verified by the sign of the empty tomb and by the reality of the apostles' encounters with the risen Christ, still it remains at the very heart of the mystery of faith as something that transcends and surpasses history. (647)

As something therefore that can only be 'met' by faith, be answered by the words, 'I believe'. And what we meet in the

Resurrection, what we believe at that moment, is not just a 'fact', fact though it is, but God himself at work, revealing himself as Trinity and as the One who is wholly, almost unbelievably, 'for us'. And so, in the act of faith, we are resurrected too and become a new creature with a new memory, a new perspective, new reasons for living. We keep the Resurrection, first of all, by renewing our faith.

Gavisi sunt! 'The disciples rejoiced' (Jn 20.20). Then there's joy. We may distinguish happiness and joy. Happiness is emotional, joy spiritual. Happiness is more external, joy more internal. Happiness is more subjective, joy more objective. Happiness is a reaction, joy is a response. Happiness is ephemeral, joy lasts. *Chairete*, Rejoice! says Jesus as he rises. The Resurrection of Jesus is joy. It is that joy greater than any that has ever been or ever will be in the history of mankind. I will see you again and your hearts will rejoice, and no one will take your joy from you. (Jn 16.22). The Resurrection is the irruption of God's joy into our life, the beginning of a joy that will last. And so, no wonder that 'the disciples were glad when they saw the Lord' (Jn 20.20). May we be too! This joy is a calm recognition of the presence of definitive salvation and ultimate good. It expresses itself in gratitude, in praise of God, in blessing God, and maybe in tears, the compunction of joy. For Guerric of Igny, the Resurrection brings a resurrection of soul now and of the body hereafter. And the resurrection of soul is itself twofold. First, there's the more fundamental grace of being raised from the death of sin 'by the operation of the mystery', and that can happen any day. But also there's a grace associated specifically with Easter: rising 'from the sleep of torpor thanks to a fervour full of joy'.[1] This is a joy which revives us and warms us up in spirit, wholly. Easter is a rekindling of spirit, a re-energizing, and it's the joy of the thing that does it. 'It is truly right and fitting etc to praise you at every season, but on this day especially to proclaim You more gloriously.' 'Blessed be the God and Father of our Lord Jesus Christ!' cries St Peter. 'By his great mercy we have been born anew to a living hope through the resurrection of Jesus Christ from the dead' (1 Pet 1.3). At the very least, a heart full of Easter will want to say thank you!

Vivendo teneant! 'May we hold on to this in our lives!'
(Prayer of Easter Monday). Finally, the Resurrection is for
living, for being 'held' by a risen life. By baptism, we die and
rise again, and every aspect of the Christian life bears this
mark. Every activity or attitude or virtue that hopefully marks
the Christian is a form of living out the Resurrection, of being
a risen person. Faith is a resurrection, so is hope, so is love,
especially love of the naturally unlovable or positively hateful.
Prayer is rising above ourselves into God. Obedience is rising
above ourselves, so is patience, so is mortification. And so
on. The Christian lives in Christ, in the once crucified, now
Risen One, and he becomes an icon of the Resurrection, even
helping raise the world – as we see in the saints. The monk,
in particular, has been called 'the icon of the Risen One'.[2]
This doesn't mean he is a superman, strutting through the day
on the stilts of his virtues. The Risen One has wounds, after
all, and he works (prefers to work, it seems) in weakness, in
oldness, in the wearying persistence of all that remains unre-
deemed within us. The resurrection of fear-free love comes
out of the death of humility, says St Benedict, and humility
comes out of humiliations (in part at least). But he is the Risen
One, and it is always resurrection that he brings. 'It is always
Easter for us', just as surely as our life should always have a
Lenten character. 'There is a living force in the faithful,'
wrote F. X. Durrwell, 'which is the principle of holy actions,
the same force that dwells in the body of the risen Christ
whereby the faithful live. The risen Christ is the principle of
Christian morality.'[3] If we can see the risen Christ in others,
we can be sure he's in ourselves, however unrisen we sometimes feel. Like recognizes like.

Easter is the time for falling in love again with the beauty
of the life in Christ. Think of the constant imagery of physical movement, of going, walking, running, in so much of what
we hear in Easter week. The women run from the empty
tomb, Peter and the beloved disciple run towards it, the two
disciples meet Jesus 'on the road' and after the meeting immediately turn round and go back to Jerusalem, Peter jumps out

of the boat in his rush to get to the shore. 'Go and tell my brethren to go to Galilee,' (Mt 28.10) says Jesus, where he is going before them. 'Do not hold me, for I have not yet ascended to the Father, but go to my brethren . . .' (Jn 20.17). 'Go into all the world and preach the gospel to the whole creation' (Mk 16.15). 'As the Father has sent me, even so I send you' (Jn 20.21). And then the cripple at the Beautiful Gate of the Temple, an icon of man raised up. Peter said:

> 'I have no silver and gold, but I give you what I have; in the name of Jesus Christ of Nazareth, walk.' And he took him by the right hand and raised him up; and immediately his feet and ankles were made strong. And leaping up he stood and walked and entered the temple with them, walking and leaping and praising God.
>
> (Acts 3.6–8)

St Paul gives the inner meaning: 'We were buried therefore with him by baptism into death, so that as Christ was raised from the dead by the glory of the Father, we too might *walk* in newness of life' (Rom 6.4).

Jesus Christ is risen from the dead. May we keep the feast – 'Easter the beautiful' – by faith, by joy, by the whole of our lives: *believing, rejoicing, living*. And may he bring us altogether to eternal life!

Notes

1. Guerric of Igny, *Sermon on the Resurrection* 3.1.
2. Article on the theme by Fr Donato, *La Scala*, April 2002.
3. F. X. Durrwell, *The Resurrection* (Sheed & Ward, New York, 1960), p. 244.

16

The Celebration of Easter

Seven Thoughts

*The Pasch of the Lord! The Pasch! Let me say it a third
time to honour the Trinity: the Pasch! For us this is the
feast of feasts, the celebration of celebrations, outshining
not only human feasts or the feasts of nature, but even
the other feasts of Christ – outshining them as the sun
outshines the stars.*[1]

I feel very strongly that the greatest public service a monastic
community can perform for itself, for the local church, for the
world as a whole, is the celebration of Easter. A full, sincere,
intelligent, prayerful celebration. Proof of this is Pannonhalma
Monastery in Hungary. As previously mentioned, under the
Communists, Catholic schools were closed, catechesis was
forbidden. The monastery, however, survived, and its annual
celebration of Holy Week and Easter drew young people from
all over the country. And it was through the Easter liturgy that
the Christian faith was handed on. And marvellous things
happened. For example, the foundation of a heroic, clandestine community of Cistercian nuns, which has now emerged.
And in its quieter way, our celebration of Easter performs a
similar service: for ourselves and the guests and the local
people at the visible level and, we trust, for others invisibly.
And so, of course, the greatest favour we can do ourselves is
open ourselves to what is being celebrated. One of the great
thrusts of Vatican II, as we know, was to bring the people
back to the liturgy and the liturgy back to the people: that it
really be the 'source and summit' of the Christian life for each

and all. And it also stressed that the paschal mystery is the centre. So the whole effort of liturgical renewal was a cry to each and all to allow the paschal mystery to be the centre and the meaning and the joy of our lives. This leads to my second thought.

The prayer for Saturday of Week 5 of Lent opens: 'Lord God, at all times you are working out the salvation of man, but now more especially you enrich your people with grace.' A lovely thought. Lent and Easter, the Triduum and the fifty days: a time of more abundant grace. And so it is. There is resurrection everywhere. During the Easter Octave, we hear of the cure of the lame beggar at the Beautiful Gate. He's anonymous and compared to many of the cured in the Gospels and Acts almost nondescript. No particular character emerges. But the first readings of Mass keep bringing him before us (Wednesday to Saturday). It's the first miracle after the Ascension, the first miracle of the Church. And so he's a symbol of our resurrection. Peter 'took him by the right hand and raised him up; and immediately his feet and ankles were made strong. And leaping up he stood and walked and entered the temple with them, walking and leaping and praising God' (Acts 3.7–8).

There is resurrection everywhere. All we need is eyes for it. Mary Magdalene saw a gardener, the two disciples saw a fellow traveller, the seven disciples saw a stranger on the shore. And it was Our Lord, risen. Someone is baptized and received into the Church at Easter and says he can't get over it; even his body feels lighter. Someone returns to the sacraments after years of absence, unloads accumulated bitterness, has a sudden peace. Someone returns to his vocation after straying from it. Someone is asked to make a sacrifice and 'rises' to it amazingly, with great generosity of spirit, living 'no longer by human passion but by the will of God' (1 Pet 4.2). Someone comes as a guest, arriving distraught and despairing and leaves with light in his eyes and even laughing. Someone dies, which is a grief for the bereaved, but an entry into life for him or her. These are all real cases. But the real point is: this is the Resurrection; this is the 'more abundant grace'; this is the effectiveness of liturgy and sacraments. The hard thing, always, is not being able to see it in oneself. On which I would offer a consolation. If we can see it in others, then it is in ourselves. Our capacity to know, to see, to recognize is based, as philosophers say, on 'likeness'. It is because we are 'like' what we know, because there is a connection between us and the object of knowledge, that we can know. If I can see the Resurrection around me, it is because it is happening in me too. What should worry us is not our inability to see the Resurrection in ourselves, but any reluctance to acknowledge it in the other. If the other turns grey with my own greyness or falls victim to my amateur psychologizing, then I do need raising from the dead! Resurrection is everywhere. 'He has come back as spring comes back out of the ground, renewing the earth with life, to be a continual renewing of life in our hearts.' It's not being silly or sentimental to include the daffodils or the forsythia. There is resurrection everywhere.

A third thought: this is 'the sacramental season'. Par excellence. It is through the sacraments that resurrection happens. The hand of God was laid on the humanity of Christ lying in the tomb, and that humanity came to life. And through the sacraments Christ, as it were, hands on what was done to him by the Father. He lays his hands on us. As the Scholastics say, his human nature is the 'conjoined instrument' of his divinity – only God can raise the dead. And the sacraments are the 'separated instruments' of his divinity and his glorified humanity. The sacraments are Christ now. Baptism and Confirmation: once and for all, in our past as events, but still running springs. Penance and Eucharist, often repeated, present. And not just sources of resurrection, causes, agents, efficient instrumental causes, but also, somehow, the sphere, the environment, the ambience of our life in the risen Christ. They're a floor that supports us, a net that catches us, a texture woven round us, a world we live in. One of the Easter graces is their rediscovery. Today's prayer (Low Sunday) is *ad rem*:

God of eternal compassion, each Easter you rekindle the faith of your consecrated people. Give them still greater, so that all may truly understand the waters in which they were cleansed, the Spirit by which they were reborn, the blood by which they were redeemed.

A fourth: it is the New Testament season. Only the New Testament is read in the liturgy. Let me just read the list: in the 1 year cycle of the Roman Office 1 Peter for Easter Week, a post-baptismal catechesis; then for the following weeks the Apocalypse; then, by way of a conclusion and inclusion perhaps, 1 John. At Mass, the Acts of the Apostles and the Gospel of John, and as the Easter Season comes to its climax at Pentecost more especially Chapters 14–17 of the Gospel of John. This is what the Church sets down on the table of the Word.

A fifth: this season and monastic life. There are two levels here. It has often been pointed out how much Easter, in the *Rule*, shapes the actual life of the monastery. It was far more than 'the centre of the liturgical year'. Rather, because it was the centre of the liturgical year it was the radial point of everything, in harness with the course of the natural year. So it determined the times and number of the meals (41) and the times of work and rest and *lectio* (48). So, the praying and reading, eating and sleeping, and working of the monks is affected, first of all, by the relationship to Easter. This is somewhat attenuated with us – with our unvarying annual timetable. The second level concerns Easter as the key to the meaning of the Christian monastic life. The Prologue in verse 2 speaks of us returning to God by the labour of obedience: a phrase which should be read in the light of the Parable of the Prodigal Son in Luke 15, of Paul's reflections on Adam and Christ in Romans 5, and such a saying as John 16.28: '1 came from the Father and have come into the world; again I am leaving the world and going to the Father.' The monk returns in the wake of Christ's passing over from this world to the Father. Prologue 3 speaks of us renouncing our own wills and taking up the weapons of obedience in the service of Christ, Lord and King. The pattern is precisely that of the renunciations and profession of baptism, the paschal sacrament. Prologue 50 could not be more explicit: 'Never abandoning his rule, but persevering in his teaching in the monastery until death, we shall share by patience in the sufferings of Christ, that we may deserve to be partakers also of his kingdom.'

In 4.46, we have the good work: 'to desire eternal life with all spiritual longing'. In 49.7, the monk is seen 'looking forward with the joy of spiritual longing to the holy feast of Easter'. Much could be developed from those two texts. One can hear behind them Luke 22.15–16: 'And he said to them, "I have earnestly desired to eat this passover with you before I suffer; for I tell you I shall not eat it until it is fulfilled in the kingdom of God."' Again, at the beginning of chapter 49, there's the famous throwaway: 'the life of a monk ought at all times to be Lenten in its character' – an adaptation of St Leo, the same Leo who said to us at Vigils this week, 'it is always Easter for us, if we abstain from the old leaven of vice and sin'. Always Lent, always Easter. Baptism and profession, asceticism and mysticism: everything is simply the working out of the paschal mystery in us. And everything can be, should be perceived, understood, thought of in that light. We forget that Easter is for our seeing and thinking as well as our living. And interesting to observe how many writers on monastic life – as diverse as Marmion, Bouyer, Ambrose Wathen and Charles Cummings – converge in a paschal understanding of it. I think the stomachs and muscles of St Benedict's monks at Monte Cassino in the sixth century would have agreed with them.

This leads to my next thought, which I can only sketch. *Oportebat* ... 'It was necessary that Christ should suffer and rise from the grave.' That is one of those alleluias of the Easter season where the conspiracy of text and music yield a very special beauty. *Oportebat* is the equivalent of the Greek *dei*, the famous 'must' we find in the Gospels of Luke and John, the 'must' that governs Christ's life, and into which monastic obedience, as well as life as a whole, take us. There is something that needs to be said here, said about suffering and obedience. It is remarkable that in the text of the alleluia, which modifies the Greek Scripture in two ways, the Resurrection too falls under the divine imperative, under the *oportebat*, the 'must'. I recall a logion of my novice master:

'Remember that the Resurrection was an obedience.' If when we hear the fourth step of humility, all we hear is, 'I'm being told to suffer', we're not hearing aright. We are radically mishearing. The focus of the fourth step of humility is not suffering, but, as we would say, 'coping with' suffering, or better transforming it. The key word is the Pauline word: we conquer, we are more than conquerors. And that, if you like, is how we experience the imperative of resurrection in this life.

We could bring in here what Anscar Vonier was trying to say in his little book *The Victory of Christ*. Or something that Caryll Houselander says in her book, *The Risen Christ*:

> We should not forget that Christ did not bring the suffering of his Passion to us; he brought his infinite love to us, it was we who gave the suffering to him. He gives suffering the power of his love, and therefore when we accept the suffering necessarily involved in living the Christlife in this world, we are not submerging ourselves more deeply into suffering than we need have done, but are doing something which will transform it ultimately into joy.[2]

One must go even a little further, I think. The Christ of Easter, who is the Christ we meet in the sacraments, who is Christ 'full-stop' (there is no other), is in the old Latin phrase *Christus passus*. Christ who has suffered, and through his suffering entered into glory. *Passus* is a past participle. And I don't think one is ignoring Rwanda or cancer or concentration camps or just the quantity of sheer pain in so many ordinary lives, if one says that for the one who is 'in Christ', 'suffering' already belongs to the past. It is one of those 'former things that have passed away' (Rev 21.4). Christ has conquered it. 'O death, where is thy sting?' And something like the fourth step of humility is showing us how that conquest can translate into our attitudes – in brief, by patient loving. Christ is the Resurrection. He said that to Martha before he died. And it was true then. He was the Resurrection even on the Cross. And now that he has actually risen, now the *passio* is past, he conveys his risen-ness, in which suffering belongs to the past, to the old aeon. He conveys it to us in the midst of our suffering. It was necessary to suffer; it was necessary to rise. The Easter season doesn't abolish suffering, but it can yield a surprising formula of victory. Experience teaches that help can sometimes come from unexpected quarters. A little imagination, a little lateral thinking ... and suddenly a new approach opens up.

Finally, seventhly: Easter is the season of rest, the anticipation of heaven. Rest means a deliberate refusal to be anxious. It means not allowing oneself to be perturbed. It means being patient with the processes of growth, being ready to accept the preordained measure, the slow pace and the long pause, the space between the first sheaf waved before the Lord and the full harvest. Christ rested between his death and his Resurrection. He told the Apostles to wait in the city until the Holy Spirit came upon them. Not to run away or start evangelizing. Not to make plans of their own, not to be troubled. Just to wait. Not the waiting of inertia, but the waiting of complete trust. Leading one spiritual writer to say this: 'Christ does not change, the preparation for the coming of the Spirit is the same today as two thousand years ago, whether it be for the rebirth of Christ in one soul that is in the hard winter or for the return from the grave of Christ, whose blood is shed again by the martyrs; the preparation is the same, the still, quiet mind, acceptance, and remaining close to the Mother of God, resting in her rest, while the life of the world grew within her towards the flowering of everlasting joy.'

Notes
1. St Gregory of Nazianzus, Discourse 45.
2. Caryll Houselander, *The Risen Christ* (Sheed & Ward, London, 1957).

17

'Woman, Why Are You Weeping?'

But Mary stood outside the tomb weeping.

(Jn 20.11)

Before Time spirits us away from the Garden, I'd like to linger there a last moment with Mary Magdalene, Mary of Magdala.

John's account of Jesus' appearance to her is unforgettable. Surely – I'm assuming the core historicity – she would never forget it. We're not told in the Gospels how she first met Jesus, or how he drove the 'seven demons' (Mk 16.9) out of her. We find her first as one of his companions in Galilee, then a spectator of the Crucifixion, then a witness to the burial. Of all the female companions of Jesus' last hours, she is the most mentioned. In the accounts of the events of Easter Sunday, she has priority too, and not least here in John's. She has come to the tomb, 'while it was still dark' (20.1), she finds the stone removed, runs back to tell Peter and the other disciples, and – we are left to assume – comes back to the tomb in their wake. They verify the emptiness, and go home. But Mary stays outside. In George Mackay Brown's imagining, Adam the gardener goes out into his garden, and is surprized.

> Over by the fountain a woman sat. It was early in the morning, the last star was in the sky, the sun was beginning to brighten the mountains eastward. As the light grew, I could see that the woman was weeping. Tears glittered here and there on her face.

On any other morning I would have sent such an intruder about her business.[1]

'And as she wept she stooped to look into the tomb.' 'Why she did so I don't know', says St Augustine, and wonders, was it *divino instinctu*? In any case, this begins the Transformation. First, an encounter with angels; then turning to see one she thinks the gardener; again her refrain, 'they have taken him away' (three times it comes: vv. 2, 13, 15); then the naming; her turning again, the cry 'Rabbuni'; his reply, 'Do not hold . . . but go . . . say . . . I am ascending.' And last, her obedience: she goes, she tells.

In these few moments, Mary moves from misery to mission. From misery to mission via a meeting and a message, that is the story. And though we hear no more of her, except in legend, we know that these few moments shaped the whole of her life and all her eternity.

Mary is more than herself. In chapter 20 of the Gospel of John, she's the second of three individuals, each of whom embodies the movement to faith in the Risen One. She is a type of the believer. She is *philochristos*, says St Cyril. She prefigures, says St Augustine, those who'll believe in Christ after his ascension, the Church drawn from the Gentiles. Yes, 'Mary, type of the Church, looked into the sepulchre', says St Ephrem. She is, says St Gregory the Great, the Bride. 'Who are you looking for? Whom do you seek?' is the question Christ asks at the very centre of the story. Surely that strikes the monastic heart! It called up the Song of Songs for Gregory:[2]

> Upon my bed during the night I sought him whom my soul loves; I sought him and did not find him. I will rise and go about the city, through its squares and streets; I will seek him whom my soul loves. (Song 3.1–2)

Mary, for him, is an icon of love desiring, questing, and keeping on, an icon of perseverance, of authentic holy desire only increased by delay. For 'Mary loved who turned a second time to see the sepulchre she had already looked into.' And to the Canticle he adds Isaiah: 'My soul has longed for you during the night, my spirit too, deep within me; from early morning I will keep watch for you' (Is 26.9), and the Psalmist too: 'God, my God, for you as soon as it is light I keep watch, my soul is athirst for you' (Ps 62.2). Mary, then, is the type of the Church as bride, of the Church as seeking, of the 'monastic Church' so to speak, and so of the monk or nun. 'Experience with Mary', says Guerric of Igny to his brethren.[3]

Respect and affection are what the Church has always given her, and rightly. And yet this is a story of conversion. Twice, says St John, she turns, and between the beginning and the end she is totally turned, from misery to mission. It's worth dwelling a while on the misery. 'Woman, why are you weeping . . . Woman, why are you weeping?' Let's try to enter her mind. Mary goes to the tomb and discovers it empty. There we have a datum of experience, a fact. Then she runs to Peter and says, 'They have taken the Lord out of the tomb, and we do not know where they have laid him.' There we have an interpretation of experience, of the fact: 'The body has been stolen.' 'Not only has he had to suffer all he suffered in the Passion, but now *they* (notice that!) have stolen the body.' It's the 'rational', 'realistic' interpretation based on the kind of thing people do – graves are robbed, bodies stolen. And it's that interpretation which makes her miserable. It's rooted in forgetfulness. She has forgotten whatever hints of resurrection there had been, or more than hints, in Jesus' life and words. And progressively it takes her over; it obsesses her. She repeats it, as I've said, three times.

It's never said before, in any of the Gospels, that Mary cried. But now she does. This is the last straw, this is the unkindest cut of all – as if what has happened hadn't been ghastly enough, now there's this final indignity. Strong as she is, she all but breaks. She breaks into tears, anyway; emotion wins out. She's reduced to misery. And she is wrong. She is completely wrong (a blessed experience, incidentally). She has misread the situation. She has seen in it only human nastiness.

She has been blinded, numbed by her own interpretation of the facts, by the rain of her tears. She thinks she's in dialogue with reality, in fact she's prisoner of her mind. She is, in classic monastic terms, the victim of *logismoi*, thoughts. Is not the whole warfare of the monk precisely here, and so often with thoughts like these? Either I rule them or they rule me, it is so simple! And is not our misery usually less in the external circumstances, in 'them', in the brethren, in the system, but in our interpretation, our reading, our reacting, our thoughts? Is it even possible that we are, with all our rationality, all our realism, simply wrong? 'Woman, why are you weeping?' ask the angels, asks the Lord. Bl Guerric identifies the appearing Jesus with Wisdom. The implication is that he's rescuing from folly. 'O foolish men and slow of heart!' And would it not be folly to spend our whole monastic life irritated, aggrieved, with circumstances, with others ('them'), with our own interpretation of the empty tomb of our lives, while all the time the Risen One is standing behind us, the other side of our thoughts, in the garden? Weeping in the garden, is it possibly a monastic pastime? Do I need to ask myself, Man, why are you weeping? Mary thought the situation should be changed, the body recovered. She didn't see God had changed it already.

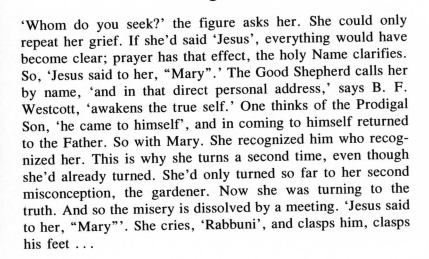

'Whom do you seek?' the figure asks her. She could only repeat her grief. If she'd said 'Jesus', everything would have become clear; prayer has that effect, the holy Name clarifies. So, 'Jesus said to her, "Mary".' The Good Shepherd calls her by name, 'and in that direct personal address,' says B. F. Westcott, 'awakens the true self.' One thinks of the Prodigal Son, 'he came to himself', and in coming to himself returned to the Father. So with Mary. She recognized him who recognized her. This is why she turns a second time, even though she'd already turned. She'd only turned so far to her second misconception, the gardener. Now she was turning to the truth. And so the misery is dissolved by a meeting. 'Jesus said to her, "Mary"'. She cries, 'Rabbuni', and clasps him, clasps his feet . . .

'Do not hold me, for I have not yet ascended to the Father; but go to my brethren and say to them, I am ascending to my Father and your Father, to my God and your God.' This verse is the climax of the whole pericope. The meeting becomes a message, and the message confers a mission.

'Do not hold me, do not cling to me, for I have not yet ascended to my Father.' Mary is still not quite there. She still misunderstands. She imagines a return to the way it used to be, the intimate, comforting times. The Fathers of the Church – preoccupied with Arianism and other heresies – will say she hadn't yet grasped his equality with the Father. The Cistercian Fathers, marked by 'the turn to the subject', will say she wasn't yet living simply by faith, her spiritual life was still at the psychic, emotional level, too dependent on experiences. She needed to ascend with the ascending Christ, to let him go and go with him (cf. Duccio).

> Become beautiful and then touch me; live by faith and you are beautiful. In your beauty you will touch my beauty all the more worthily, with greater felicity. You will touch me with the hand of faith, the finger of desire, the embrace of love; you will touch me with the mind's eye.[4]

'I have not yet ascended ... I am ascending.' The surprise is the emphasis upon Ascension, just when we'd expect festivity around the Resurrection. But isn't it completely Johannine? 'I am ascending to *the Father*.' This is the Gospel of the One who comes from the Father and goes to the Father. Resurrection, of itself, looks back. It looks back to a *terminus a quo*; it is 'resurrection *from the dead*' (cf. 20.9). More important, though, is the *terminus ad quem*, the goal of the movement, and it's that the concept of Ascension proposes. It proposes the Father. As of the Passion, so of the Resurrection, the deepest meaning is, 'I am going to the Father.' But still there's more. What Jesus is conveying here is not simply information about himself, about his personal journey. It is, beyond that, a promise of all that will follow his Ascension. So, he says, 'I am ascending to my Father and your Father, to my God and your God', the disciples now 'my (that is, his) brethren'. With his Ascension there begins a new epoch, there opens a new world, of relationships. All that was said in the Last Discourse is about to be fulfilled.

'I will not leave you desolate; I will come to you. Yet a little while, and the world will see me no more, but you will see me; because I live, you will live also. In that day you will know that I am in my Father, and you in me, and I in you' ... Judas (not Iscariot) said to him, 'Lord how is it that you will manifest yourself to us, and not to the world?' Jesus answered him, 'If a man loves me, he will keep my word, and my Father will love him, and we will come to him and make our home with him ... I tell you the truth: it is to your advantage that I go away, for if I do not go away, the Counsellor will not come to you; but if I go, I will send him to you ... When the Spirit of truth comes, he will guide you into all the truth ... He will glorify me, for he will take what is mine and declare it to you ... Truly, truly I say to you, if you ask anything of the Father, he will give it to you in my name. Hitherto you have asked nothing in my name; ask, and you will receive, that your joy may be full.'

(Jn 14.18–20, 22–3; 16.7, 13, 14, 23–24)

It is through his Ascension that all this glory will be opened to the disciples, and they will be able to enter into it, 'that the love with which you have loved me may be in them, and I in them'. It is through his Ascension that all the glories that a Catholic theology of grace stutters to articulate will be conveyed. It is through his Ascension that the Church, in its most essential reality, as a brotherhood in Christ, will come into being. It is through his Ascension that the Spirit will come and prayer in Christ begin.

Irresistible here are the words Newman, in his Anglican *Lectures on Justification*, puts on Our Lord's lips:

Thou hast seen Me, Mary, but couldst not hold Me; thou hast approached Me, but only to embrace My feet, or to be touched by My hand; and thou sayest, 'O that I knew where I might find Him, that I might come even to His seat! O that I might hold Him and not let Him go!' Henceforth this shall be; when I am ascended, thou shalt see nothing, thou shalt have everything. Thou shalt 'sit down under My shadow with great delight, and

My fruit shall be sweet to thy taste.' Thou shalt have Me whole
and entire. I will be near thee, I will be in thee; I will come into
thy heart a whole Saviour, a whole Christ, – in all my fullness as
God and man, – in that awful virtue of that Body and Blood,
which has been taken into the Divine Person of the Word, and is
indivisible from it, and has atoned for the sins of the world, – not
by external contact, not by partial possession, not by momentary
approaches, not by a barren manifestation, but inward in presence, and intimate in fruition, a principle of life and a seed of
immortality, that thou mayest 'bring forth fruit unto God'.[5]

So we come back to Mary and her mission. She is not sent
into the whole world, or to the whole creation. She is sent to
Christ's brethren. She is sent to the Church. There are two
simultaneous movements in play: Jesus' to the Father and
Mary's to his brethren, and they are not in conflict. As he
goes to the Father and she to the brethren, he also goes with
her to them, and she with him to the Father. It is all one. It
is a world of impossibles reconciled, of spiritual bilocation.
And she is sent to the Church, to her fellow disciples, to
announce, to be the angel (*angelousa*, says the Greek) of, the
imminent new realm of grace, of holiness, of the Spirit, of
relationship with the Father and with one another in Jesus. She
is to proclaim its advent and by implication its beauty. And if
she is the monastic face and voice of the Church, if she is a
type of any monastic community, then she is of its mission
within the Church. In her we see its/our mission. In her we're
called to enter the Church ever more deeply, so as to be the
Church, and show forth the beauty of Christian being, Christian brotherhood, Christian life, Christian prayer, of all that
Christ's Ascension has brought to mankind. We are called to
go to the brethren carrying in ourselves, in our eyes and ears,
his going to the Father. We are called, as a monastic community, to live in the heart of the Church and by our lives
proclaim the New Covenant's fullness of grace.

With penetrating insight, the Fathers have called this spiritual
path *philokalia*, or 'love of the divine beauty', which is the reflection of the divine goodness. Those who by the power of the Holy
Spirit are led progressively into full configuration with Christ

reflect in themselves a ray of unapproachable light. During their earthly pilgrimage, they press on towards the inexhaustible Source of light. The consecrated life thus becomes a particularly profound expression of the Church as the Bride who, prompted by the Spirit to imitate her Spouse, stands before him 'in splendour, without spot or wrinkle or any such thing, that she might be holy and without blemish' (Eph 5.27).[6]

Such a mission will have its suffering – according to Mk 16.11, it was at first rejected – but it is Mary's and our deliverance from misery.

From misery to mission, then; from misery to mission via a meeting and a message. It's not a movement we make once and for all; we make it daily, every day, in the garden of the Resurrection which the monastery is. Every day, we need to be turned from living in our minds, from subjective assessments, from interpretations not of God, from meaningless miseries. Every day, we need to be turned back to our mission, to the priority of seeking holiness, in daily work, daily prayer, in the heart of the Church. And every day it can happen, because, as Guerric says again, what he did corporally on Easter day 'he does not cease to do spiritually day by day'. Every day, he says my name, and calls me back to my true self, away from *logismoi*. Every day, he comes with a word and himself (the Liturgy of the Word, of the Eucharist; *lectio*, prayer). Every day he says, 'Go to my brethren'; every day, 'I am ascending to my Father and to your Father, to my God and to your God.'

Notes
1. George Mackay Brown, *The Rose Tree 7* (Celtic Cross Press, York, 2001).
2. St Gregory the Great, *Homilies on the Gospels*, 25.
3. Guerrric of Igny, Sermon 3 *for Easter*, 2.
4. St Bernard, *On the Song of Songs*, 28:10.
5. Newman, *Lectures on Justification*, IX, 8.
6. John Paul II, *Vita Consecrata* 19.

18

The Spiritual Presence of Christ

This, indeed, is our state at present; we have lost Christ and we have found Him; we see Him not, yet we discern Him. We embrace His feet, yet He says, 'Touch me not'. How is this? It is thus: we have lost the sensible and conscious perception of Him; we cannot look on Him, hear Him, converse with Him, follow Him from place to place; but we enjoy the spiritual, immaterial, inward, mental, real sight and possession of Him; a possession more real and more present than that which the Apostles had in the days of His flesh, because it is spiritual, because it is invisible.[1]

So preached Newman in his sermon *The Spiritual Presence of Christ in the Church*, words apposite to this time of the liturgical year.

If the Resurrection is one object of attention during the fifty days of Easter, and the life of the Church another, so too, bringing the two together, is the 'spiritual presence of Christ in the Church'. On the Fourth Sunday of Easter, we hear about the Good Shepherd. He knows his own and calls them by name and leads them out to pasture. He is present among us, our Shepherd. He gives his life daily for us in the Eucharist. On the Fifth Sunday, the Gospels are all taken from the Last Discourse of John, chapters 13ff. 'I am the Way, the Truth and the Life' (Year A); 'I am the vine, you are the branches' (Year B); 'I give you a new commandment: love one another' (Year C). All these Gospels keep us aware of the

closeness of Christ: his presence in the Church as a whole, as
a single entity, and his presence to each and every member of
the Church.

> Christ has promised He will be with us to the end, – be with us,
> not only as He is in the unity of the Father and the Son, not in
> the Omnipresence of the Divine Nature, but personally, as the
> Christ, as God and man; not present with us locally and sensibly,
> but still really, in our hearts and to faith. And it is by the Holy
> Ghost that this gracious communion is effected. How he effects it
> we know not; in what precisely it consists we know not. We see
> Him not; but we are to believe that we possess Him, – that we
> have been brought under the virtue of His healing hand, of His
> life-giving breath, of the manna flowing from His lips, and of the
> blood flowing from His side.[2]

On St Mark's day we heard this from St Cyril of Alexandria:

> The one foundation, the unshakable support of the universe is
> Christ, who upholds all things, and preserves in well-being all
> that has been firmly founded. We are all built upon him: we are
> a spiritual house bonded together by the Spirit to form a holy
> temple which is his own dwelling-place, for he dwells in our
> hearts through faith.[3]

The great means by which Christ is present to his Church and
in our lives is the sacraments, especially the sacraments of
Baptism, Confirmation and the Eucharist. And this 'economy'
cries out for consideration at this time of the year. Lent and
Easter form the sacramental season par excellence. Maundy
Thursday is almost overloaded with sacramental allusions:
reconciliation, priesthood, the oils, the institution of the
Eucharist. The paschal Vigil renews our baptism. The Gospel
of Low Sunday includes the words: 'Receive the Holy Spirit.
For those whose sins you forgive, they are forgiven; for those
whose sins you retain, they are retained.' During the second
week of Easter, the Gospel readings are taken from John
chapter 3, Jesus' conversation with Nicodemus: 'I tell you
most solemnly, unless a man is born through water and the

Spirit, he cannot enter the kingdom of God.' Then they turn to John chapter 6: 'He who eats my flesh and drinks my blood lives in me and I live in him.' The fifty days of Easter are, as a whole, a time of mystagogy, for being inducted into the meaning of the sacraments, and Pentecost itself is a reminder of our Confirmation.

Yes, surely, it is above all in the sacramental actions of the Church that the risen and ascended Christ is active among us. His human nature, by virtue of the Incarnation, became the 'conjoined instrument' of his divinity, and therefore able to save us. The sacraments are, as it were, a further extension of his humanity, 'separated instruments', but instruments nonetheless. They are the tools, as it were, of Jesus' trade, the extensions of his hands. During his life on earth, he took Peter's mother-in-law by the hand and raised her up. Now in glory, he does the same spiritually through the priest who baptizes or absolves or anoints. The acts of power recorded in the Gospels are signs and anticipations of the sacramental action of the risen Christ. 'What was visible in our Saviour,' as St Leo famously said, 'has passed over into his mysteries.' And just as it was possible to overlook Christ in his earthly life, just as it's possible to overlook him as a historical figure or to reckon him no more than a Jewish Confucius or Buddha or Muhammad or Marx or Freud, so it is possible to overlook the sacramental Christ. The sacraments, actually, are very unspectacular. They involve ordinary things, water, oil, bread, wine, usually in small quantities. They involve simple actions like pouring (or at the most dunking), anointing, touching, speaking, eating, drinking. They generally don't require a great amount of time. In a monastery, the Mass, for example, may usually be celebrated with a certain style, with a liturgical haute couture, but we all know how plain, swift and simple a Mass can be. There can almost be a sense of anti-climax; at least there's a disproportion between what is claimed for any of the sacraments and how they actually come across. Experientially, too. Someone's interior life can become detached from the sacraments. Yes, it is easy to overlook them. Yet they are, says the *Catechism* (1116), '"powers that come forth" from the body of Christ, which is ever-living and life-giving. They are actions of the Holy Spirit at work in his Body, the Church. They are "the masterworks of God" in the new and everlasting covenant.' And, says Nicholas Cabasilas, 'The holy life is brought about by the sacred Mysteries.'[4]

Rudyard Kipling had one son, John, who was killed early and young in the First World War. In July 1914, just before the war, he had been baptized of his own will, not having been such as a child, and no doubt wanting something better than his father's own idiosyncratic hotchpotch of agnosticism, religion and spirituality. In September 1915, he was killed at the Battle of Loos. Is it superstitious to see in that baptism Christ's providential blessing on that young man? Anyway, Rudyard's biographer makes no such connection, and only expresses regret that this young man does not appear to have lost his virginity to the pretty French daughter of the family with whom he was billeted. It's easy to overlook the sacraments. How often do even biographies of saints connect the total lives of their subjects with their sacramental lives? And yet Christ and his Spirit are present in those lives, above all, by means of the sacraments.

A seminarian once wrote to me: could he make his retreat before ordination to the diaconate here, so as to reflect on 'the commitment' he was about to make? But it's a sacrament before it's a commitment. Columba Marmion once made a retreat simply around the sacraments he had received, re-reading and re-praying day by day the different rites he had undergone. It is good to look at our lives, our own biography, through the lenses of the sacraments.

Think of baptism. It's a seed planted in us when we are young, very young perhaps, and like the seed of the Gospel, while the child 'sleeps and rises night and day ... the seed sprouts and grows, he knows not how. The earth produces of itself, first the blade, then the ear, then the full grain in the ear' (Mk 4.27–28). 'It is like a grain of mustard seed, which, when sown upon the ground, is the smallest of all the seeds on the earth; yet when it is sown it grows up and becomes the greatest of all shrubs, and puts forth large branches, so that the birds of the air can make nests in its shade' (Mk 4.31–32).

So it is with Christian Baptism. Nothing shows, for some time, that the Spirit of God is come into, and dwells in the child baptized; it looks like any other child, it is pained, it frets, is weak, is wayward, like any other child; for 'the Lord seeth not as man seeth' . . . [Yet] sooner or later that work of God is manifested, which was at first secret'.[5]

The branches of our monastic life spring from the baptismal seed.

Another image: a well sunk into us, or rather opened up for us. 'The water that I shall give him will become in him a spring of water welling up to eternal life' (Jn 4.14), as Jesus said by the well of Sychar. Whenever the water of grace is running through our lives, it's springing up from the baptismal well. Or again, if baptism is a share in the death and Resurrection of Christ, as Paul says it is in Romans 6, then it establishes a pattern. It is something like a filter for the whole of our experience, or shapes us, as it were, like a mould into which the molten metal of life is poured and thereby 'paschalized'. The baptismal sequence of death and resurrection is repeated throughout our pilgrimage. Down we go, sometimes, into the death-dealing waters, but up we come by the power of God. Baptismal grace, if we pay heed to it, 'remember' it, converts a situation of death into one of resurrection. My baptism is an element of my present, not just of my past.

'Let the children come to me, do not hinder them' (Mk 10.14). It is a beautiful thing to have been baptized as a child. It means that Christ has looked at me and loved me and laid his hand on me. It means that he was there from the beginning. It is a sign of God's prevenient love. As the *Catechism* says: 'the sheer gratuitousness of the grace of salvation is particularly manifest in infant Baptism' (1250). The whole theology of the sacramental character reinforces this: I am marked, sealed, stamped, branded as belonging to God in Christ; nothing can wipe this out. There's great consolation to be had in this.

At confirmation, in turn, Christ breathes the Holy Spirit into me: 'Be sealed with the Gift of the Holy Spirit.' And so Christ himself becomes present to me and in me in a new way.

I think it is often after we have received the gift of the Holy
Spirit in confirmation that our particular Christian path begins
to open up. Again, it is easy to overlook the connections. The
fact is, though, that in her Canon Law, the Church requires
confirmation prior to ordination, marriage or profession. The
theological implication is that it is the Holy Spirit who distrib-
utes his gifts as he wills and who moves us to the way and the
work that Christ has predestined for us.

And then the Eucharist, the Sacrament of Sacraments, and
the presence of Christ, not merely in action and transitorily,
but 'really, truly and substantially'. The sacrament of union
and intimacy, and therefore probably the most overlooked, the
most abused. I can remember some time after becoming a
Catholic wanting to receive the Eucharist more than the twice
a week recommended by the priest who received me. I asked
him about it, and he encouraged me, and so I began to go to
Mass daily so far as possible. What this then releases into
one's life! In retrospect, it seems to me a crucial step.

All this requires, of course, our co-operation. We have to
respond, as all the spiritual teachers say. The sacraments
involve our own faith and effort. Yes. But, as in the Church
as a whole, so in my own life, it is Christ who is first, the
Beginning. It is grace that is first. It's God who's the subject
of the sentence. It's God who gives us the Christ-life. He
begets it, inspires it, nourishes and perfects it, restores it,
repairs it. We are his workmanship, and that by way of the
tools of his good works, the sacraments.

St Ambrose, St Cyril of Jerusalem, and other Fathers too,
took pains to explain to the newly-baptized the grace they had
been given through the 'mysteries'. We as old hands can echo
that mystagogy on ourselves, especially at this time of the
year, the sacramental season, when everything reminds us of
Christ's presence among us.

Let me end with some words on Holy Communion from
Nicholas Cabasilas:

> After the Chrismation we go to the table. This is the perfection
> of the life in Christ; for those who attain it there is nothing
> lacking for the blessedness which they seek. It is no longer death

and the tomb and a participation in the better life which we receive, but the risen One himself. Nor do we receive such gifts of the Spirit as we may, but the very Benefactor himself, the very Temple on which is founded the whole range of graces.

Now indeed Christ is present in each of the Mysteries. It is with Himself that we are anointed and washed; He also is our feast. He is present with those who are being initiated and imparts his gifts to them ... But when he has led the initiate to the table and has given him his Body to eat he entirely changes him, and transforms him into his own state ... It is impossible to conceive of anything more blessed than this ...

When Christ dwells in us, what else is needed, or what benefit escapes us? When we dwell in Christ, what else will we desire? He dwells in us, and He is our dwelling place ...

O how great are the mysteries! What a thing it is for Christ's mind to be mingled with ours, our will to be blended with his, our body with his Body and our blood with his Blood! What is our mind when the divine mind obtains control? What is our will when that blessed will has overcome it? What is our dust when it has been overpowered by his fire?

To sum it all up, 'it is no longer I who live, but Christ lives in me' (Gal 2.20).[6]

Notes

1. Newman, *Parochial and Plain Sermons*, 6, 10, p. 121.
2. Ibid., pp. 133–4.
3. St Cyril of Alexandria, *In Is*.
4. Nicolas Cabasilas, *The Life in Christ*, 11, 1.
5. Newman, Ibid., 8, 4, pp. 57–8.
6. Cabasilas, IV, 1–2.

19

'Come, Holy Spirit!'

Pentecost Homily 2001

Sunday today brings us Pentecost, Whitsun. In the winter, we have Christmas. In spring, Easter. And now in summer, Whitsun, Pentecost: the third of the three great feasts of the year, the rounding-off of the fifty days of Easter, their completion, and a fullness for us.

What we celebrate at Pentecost, first of all, is the event we heard of in the first Reading from the Acts of the Apostles (2.1–11). It is fifty days after the Resurrection of Jesus, ten days after his Ascension, and on the Jewish feast of Pentecost the Apostles are all together in Jerusalem, waiting as Jesus had told them to do. Then suddenly the Holy Spirit comes upon them. He makes himself audible, first, with a sound like a powerful wind. He makes himself visible in something like tongues of fire, coming to rest on the head of each of them. This is a theophany, a manifestation of God. And then, within themselves, 'they were all filled with the Holy Spirit': filled to the full, in body, soul and spirit, in mind and heart and will, filled with the power of God. Perhaps we think back to the Annunciation to Mary, set at the beginning of the Gospel, the story of Christ, as this is set at the beginning of the Acts, the story of the Church. 'How can this be?' Mary had asked. And the angel replied, 'The Holy Spirit will come upon you, and the power of the Most High will overshadow you' (Lk 1.34, 35). And so Mary, giving her consent, was filled body, soul and spirit, with the Holy Spirit, with the power of God: 'And the Word was made flesh and dwelt among us.'

Now the same Holy Spirit comes down on the Twelve, and

the Word becomes flesh in another way. They 'began to speak foreign languages as the Spirit gave them the gift of speech'. They were able to proclaim the Gospel, the word of God, in such a way that the crowds up at Jerusalem for the feast can hear this word in their own different languages: 'Parthians, Medes and Elamites; people from Mesopotamia, Judaea and Cappadocia and so on, visitors from Rome – Jews and prose-lytes alike – Cretans and Arabs.' The preaching of the truth of Christ has begun, and the gathering of the nations into the Church. Already at Pentecost, the Church is catholic, the Church is one, and the re-gathering of scattered humanity is underway. The Holy Spirit filled a Virgin from Galilee, and the body of Christ began to grow in her womb. Thirty years on, at Pentecost, the Holy Spirit fills twelve men from Galilee, and the body of Christ begins to grow in the world. This is what we remember today.

But it isn't only that. It's clear from the second reading (1 Cor 12: 3–7, 12–13) that another almost thirty years on, in a new Christian generation, the Spirit was still being given: given for the profession of faith, 'Jesus is Lord'; given in baptism and confirmation; given in the variety of personal gifts that build up the body of Christ. And so it is, generation after generation, and day after day. Every day at every Mass, the Holy Spirit comes down on the bread and wine as he came on the womb of Mary and changes them into the body and blood of Christ, changing us too who receive them into the one same body. It is the whole life-giving, life-changing pres-ence of the Holy Spirit in the Church and in our lives that we remember and give thanks for today. Without the Holy Spirit we are capable of nothing in the supernatural life.

> If Thou withdraw Thy breath, forthwith my three mortal enemies rush on me and overcome me. I am weak as water, I am utterly impotent without thee. The minute thou dost cease to act in me, I begin to languish, to gasp and to faint away.[1]

But with the Holy Spirit, we are capable, capable especially of transcending ourselves and loving where love seems impos-sible. By the grace of God, Pentecost isn't just a day in the past; it isn't just one day in the year. It is, as the Collect says, *nunc quoque*, now too, now as well, any now, any minute, any day, any generation. And it's that we celebrate too.

But there is one more thing. Christmas, Easter, Pentecost. There is a sequence here. There is an unfolding of God. The Father gives the Son, first of all. He gives him at Christmas, the Word was made flesh, a Virgin gives birth. He gives him at Easter, the tomb is found empty. And then the Father and the Son together give the Spirit: Pentecost and now. And God has literally nothing more to give. Having given the Spirit he has given us everything: in faith for the present, the vision for heaven. The Spirit is the love that unites the Father and the Son, and the love that unites us to the Father and to the Son. If the Father is the house to which we are travelling, the Son is the door, but the Spirit is the key. And today we are given the key. If the Father is the goal and the Son the way, then the Spirit is one who guides us on the way, our travel guide. If the Father is God above us and the Son God beside us, the Spirit is God within us. Everything that could be given has been given. We are Christians, and as Christians we believe in the Father, the Son and the Holy Spirit. Today we can say that. Today we know God. And thanks to Pentecost there is nothing left for us to do but enter in. 'Give us comfort when we die; Give us life with thee on high; Give us joys that never end.' Amen.

Note
1. Newman, *Prayers and Meditations*, XIV.

20

Mary Assumed into Heaven

The Assumption of Mary, which we celebrate on 15 August –
Our Lady in harvest time, the corn gathered in – is both a
beginning and an end. '[I]n the glory which she possesses in
body and soul in heaven, [she] is the image and *beginning* of
the Church as it is to be perfected in the world to come,' says
Lumen Gentium 68. Taken up into heaven, she assumes, she
begins, in a new way, her role of intercessor, of mother in the
order of grace. At the same time, as when anyone passes from
this world to the Father, it is natural to look back at her whole
life, re-reading it in the light of her end. Whichever way we
look, it seems to me, we see the centrality of prayer, her
prayer. We see her as a person of prayer, as the *Orans* par
excellence. And we see this prayer not just as something she
does for us from the outside, as it were, but something which
can shape our own prayer from within; as a prayer which it is
possible for us to share in, commune with. Her prayer, in
some sense, is our prayer, her Magnificat our Magnificat.
'For in the mystery of the Church, which is rightly called a
mother and a virgin, says *Lumen Gentium* again, the Blessed
Virgin Mary has gone ahead (*praecessit*)' (62), that is, she has
been an example for us to follow. And if in being 'Church',
so also in prayer, allowing us to say with St Ambrose: 'Let
the soul of Mary be in each person to magnify the Lord, let
the spirit of Mary be in each person to exult in God.'[1] That's
really what I want to say: that Mary's prayer can rescue and
enrich our own.

The mind can be a nuisance – or at least mine can – and so,

thinking along these lines, I ended up with the tenfold prayer of Mary, beginning with the prayer of the Immaculate and ending with the prayer of the Assumed. But I'll only dwell on three or four of them! Let me remove an objection first, though, with a sentence of Fr Raniero Cantalamessa: 'The Magnificat is Mary's because the Holy Spirit attributed it to her and this makes it more 'hers' than if she had actually written it herself.'[2] This can be applied to the whole New Testament portrait of Mary and to every word she's shown saying. There's no need to worry, in a nervous, modern way: did she actually do this, say this? The Holy Spirit, inspiring the Evangelists, has given us a picture of Mary which is true to her. Only the Holy Spirit could.

Let me begin with the prayer of the Immaculate. Mary, we believe, was conceived immaculate, without the stain of original sin. This was something that affected her ontologically, as they say, at the depths of her being, in her relation to God, and did so from the very first moment of her existence. And, with the passage of time, in infancy perhaps, certainly in early childhood – St Thérèse was consciously relating to the Lord from the age of three – and then onwards through the whole of her life, this root of original grace would have borne the flower and fruit of an immaculate prayer. It's good for the soul to think of this, however clumsily. The grace of our baptism, for all our neglect of it, for all the residue of concupiscence, still puts us in sympathy with the grace of an immaculate conception. Thanks to her original grace, Mary faced God-wards always. We might call it *the prayer of* the *presence of God*. What St Benedict proposes on the first step of humility, the keeping of the fear of God before one's eyes, or what Br Lawrence called the practice of the presence of God, or what the spiritual writers call the prayer of simple regard or simple recollection, not to mention things more infused and mystical, must have all pre-existed in Mary in a way very simple, uncomplicated, whole and entire. The new Eve never hid herself among the trees.

There are hints of this in the liturgy of 8 December, in the responsory from the Book of Wisdom 7.25: *candor est lucis aeternae et speculum sine macula*, 'she is a reflection of

eternal light, a spotless mirror of the working of God', or in
the antiphon inspired by the Transfiguration: *facies tua sicut
sol*, 'your face is like the sun'. Her face was like the sun,
because it was turned to the sun. She woke up facing God-
wards, conscious of His presence, and she lived every day
within it. Psalm 139, 'O Lord, thou hast searched me and
known me!', was more hers than anyone's. 'Thou knowest
when I sit down and when I rise up; thou discernest my
thoughts from far away ... For thou didst form my inward
parts, thou didst knit me together in my mother's womb. I
praise thee, for thou art fearful and wonderful. Wonderful are
thy works!' (Ps 139.1–2,13–14). And flowing from this surely
everything that the spiritual tradition of the Church says about
the 'contemplation of things created' must have been verified
in her; the transparency a great painter can evoke (like
Vermeer and his maid pouring milk) must have been habitual.
No thing, no action, no event without light shining through it.
Conversely, no wrenching, no grinding gears, in the daily
traffic between the created and the Creator. And correspond-
ingly the free passage that phrases from Scripture or touches
of grace must have had in her heart, or the unmuffled impact
of the words of her Son. And then yet again, how this prayer
must have made her vulnerable to suffering even while
enabling her to bear it. All this is stammering, of course. But
though 'fools rush in' and so on rings in the ears or, simply,
warnings against sentimental psychologizing, the prayer of
Mary Immaculate doesn't seem to me an inappropriate subject
of contemplation. It may mean no more (and no less) than
looking at a Gospel phrase like, 'Behold, I am the handmaid
of the Lord' (Lk 1.38), and wondering where it came from.
In fact, everything that the Gospels of St Luke and St John
record Mary as saying is either prayer or the fruit of prayer.
The holy Anglican bishop Thomas Ken (d. 1711) once said of
an infant, 'It's such a delight to look at a being that has never
wilfully offended its Maker.' And so with Mary: it's refresh-
ment and delight to look at someone who not only never
wilfully offended, but was always a mirror without blemish,
always a delight to the Father. 'And I was daily his delight,
rejoicing before him always' (Prov 8.31).

Somewhere there perhaps is a first facet of Mary's prayer, the prayer that came from her immaculate conception and is waiting too within us, at our level, thanks to the original grace of our baptism, continually renewed by the Holy Spirit. It's the prayer of someone who knows they're living in the presence of Another. May Mary, conceived without sin, guide us into that prayer and hold us there.

Well, the Angel came, and Mary said, 'Let it be done to me according to your word' (Lk 1.38), the *prayer of acceptance*. There's the visit to Elizabeth, and Mary's soul 'proclaims the greatness of the Lord', the *prayer of praise*. There's the birth of her child, and St Luke's double reference to her heart: 'But Mary kept all these things, pondering them in her heart'; 'and his mother kept all these things in her heart' (Lk 2.19, 51). This is the *prayer of meditation*, *ruminatio*, the prayer of a motherly heart, prayer seeking to understand. And then we shouldn't forget the Temple and its liturgy: 'Now his parents went to Jerusalem every year at the feast of the Passover' (Lk 2.41). This is festive, *ritual prayer*. It's another strand. Then, one year, 'Son, why have you treated us so? Behold, your father and I have been looking for you anxiously' (Lk 2.48). It's the *prayer of anguish and bewilderment*.

But let me pause at Cana in Galilee. 'When the wine failed, the mother of Jesus said to him: "They have no wine"' (Jn 2.3). The *prayer of compassion*. What is immediately striking is the turning to Jesus the moment the need is perceived. 'The mother of Jesus said to him ...' I suppose the hosting family would never have lived down that failure of wine at the wedding; it would have been passed down in the village's gossip from generation to generation. And Mary turns to Jesus, simply presents him with the lack, doesn't initiate anything herself except the appeal to her Son. Here surely, if anywhere, those called to the contemplative life can say to themselves, 'Let the soul of Mary be in each of us ... Let the spirit of Mary be in each of us.' What can we do, when we see or hear of the world's lack of wine, and feel it in ourselves, in our own poverty, except appeal to Jesus? 'They have no wine': lives without joy or even hope of joy. 'They have no wine': no awareness that there is such a thing as the wedding of the Lamb and a new covenant and a new cup and a new song. 'They have no wine': no knowledge of redemption. It's not our job directly to work for social justice or to evangelize. We just have to say, 'They have no wine'. And this not out of condescension, but compassion; just a simple turning to Jesus and a minimum of words. And with Mary's sensitivity. A situation is shown us, a need, and it is a call to prayer. Again, I think, Cana doesn't simply look to Mary praying for us now, asking wine from her Son for poor humanity, but it looks to us, too, praying after her.

'Standing by the cross of Jesus were his mother, and his mother's sister, Mary the wife of Clopas, and Mary Magdalene' (Jn 19.25). This is prayer beside the Cross, a prayer still sustained by original grace and the acceptance of the original motherhood, but now just turned to suffering. And Mary says nothing.

> We know that the whole creation has been groaning in travail together until now; and not only the creation, but we ourselves, who have the first fruits of the Spirit, groan inwardly as we wait for adoption as sons, the redemption of our bodies ... Likewise the Spirit helps us in our weakness; for we do not know how to pray as we ought, but Spirit himself intercedes for us with sighs too deep for words. (Rom 8.22–23, 26)

That might be one glimpse of what was going on in Mary. Another would be a woman's description of St Teresa Benedicta of the Cross (Edith Stein) in the Dutch detention camp at Westerbork:

> What distinguished Edith from the rest ... was her silence. Rather than seeming fearful, to me she appeared deeply oppressed. Maybe the best way I can explain it is to say that she carried so much pain that it hurt to see her smile. She hardly ever spoke; but often she would look at her sister Rosa with a sorrow beyond words.[3]

Jesus, though, does have words for his mother: 'Woman,

behold your son!' (Jn 19.26), and the next sight of Mary that
we have, from St Luke at the beginning of Acts, is in a sense
a commentary on it: 'All these [the Eleven] with one accord
devoted themselves to prayer, together with the women and
Mary the mother of Jesus, and with his brethren' (Acts 1.14).
It's striking that Mary, so to speak, leaves the New Testament
praying, just as we imagine her assumed into heaven praying
for us. We could call Mary's prayer here the *prayer of the
Church*. It is persevering, unanimous prayer, now directed
through the risen and ascended Christ and asking for the Holy
Spirit to come and fill the Church of God. And Mary disappears into it: led by the Eleven, surrounded by the other
women and the brethren of Jesus. This is Christian liturgy
beginning. This is the Church begging for the Holy Spirit and
becoming a mother. This is Mary's spiritual motherhood,
received by the Cross, now bearing fruit. It's another facet of
her prayer and therefore of ours.

By the grace of the Assumption, this prayer continues in
heaven, the *prayer of intercession*, and we can continue it on
earth in harmony with Mary. Nothing I've seriously asked her
for, or asked her to ask for, at the end of Compline has been
refused me.

There's a phrase that haunts me, and I'd be happy for it to
haunt every one of us: *domus mea, domus orationis vocabitur*,
'My house shall be called a house of prayer' (Is 56.7; Mt
21.13). That house is the Temple, the Church, Mary, the
monastery, each of us. 'My house shall be called a house of
prayer.' That's our 'vocation'. *Ecclesia in Europa*, the 2003
Post-Synodal Exhortation of John Paul II, says this: 'There is
a need for communities which, by contemplating and imitating the Virgin Mary, the figure and model of the Church in
faith and holiness, cultivate the sense of liturgical life and of
interior life' (27). May we be such! May Mary's prayer come
to the rescue and enrichment of ours; root it in the Church,
make it compassionate, keep it in the truth of God's Presence;
give it some share in the splendour and depth of her own. May
the spirit of Mary, assumed into heaven, be in each of us to

magnify the Lord, and the soul of Mary be in each of us to exult in God our Saviour.

Notes

1. St Ambrose, *In Lucam* II, 26.
2. Fr Raniero Cantalamessa, *The Mystery of Christmas* (St Paul's, Slough, 1988), p. 9.
3. W. Herbstrith, *Edith Stein* (Ignatius, San Francisco, 1992), p. 182.

21

With All the Saints

Homily 2004

Today we are glorifying God, the holy God, Father, Son and Holy Spirit, for all those believers now in heaven: standing victorious in front of the Throne and the Lamb; seeing God as he really is; comforted, satisfied, shown mercy; praying for us; a large number, impossible to count, of people from every nation, race, tribe and language.

This is the vision, the corner of the curtain pulled back, the glimpse through the window which we are shown today; the feast of All Saints.

'I, John, saw' (Rev 7.2): the first three words of the first of today's three readings, from the book of the Apocalypse or Revelation. 'I, John, saw'. They're an open sesame, a hand lifting the edge of the veil. 'I, John, your brother' (1.9), not John the Evangelist it seems, but John an early Christian prophet and a seer. 'I John ... was on the island called Patmos on account of the word of God and the testimony of Jesus' (1.9), as a result, that is, of persecution. And 'in the Spirit on the Lord's day ' (1.10), 'I looked, and lo, in heaven an open door' (4.1). And among the things he saw was what we are giving God glory for today:

> a huge number, impossible to count, of people from every nation, race, tribe and language, standing in front of the throne and in front of the Lamb, dressed in white robes and holding palms in their hands. They shouted aloud, 'Victory to our God who sits on the throne, and to the Lamb!' (7.9–10)[1]

He saw the assembly of saints, he saw the Church triumphant, he saw that portion of humanity that has come through the trial of suffering, has made it home and is in joy. And this vision, among the others, was written down for the comfort of the churches; the Book of Revelation took shape. And that book, with this vision, has been recognized by the Church as canonical Scripture and placed at the end, as a climax even, of the New Testament and the whole of inspired Scripture. What that means, very simply, is that what John saw, we see. His vision is our vision. We cannot fully have heard the word of God, we cannot be fully believers, unless this vision too lights us up. The Church on earth carries in her heart images of the Church in heaven, of the Throne, of the risen Christ, of the River of the water of life, of Mary assumed into glory, of apostles and angels, prophets and martyrs and so on. And with those images in her heart she is always able to see beyond any immediate darkness, enveloping gloom. 'I, John, saw.' She is able to keep faith and hope, and keep on the move towards that waiting crowd. The Church of heaven is her hidden strength. And we are invited to share it, each of us.

Recently one of the brethren repainted the slippers and cuffs of the image of Mary we have in our church. That could be taken as a symbol for the grace of this feast. It's like dusting the iconostasis, touching up the statues, refurbishing the images.

'I was in the Spirit on the Lord's day,' said John. What that very likely means is that John had his visions at Sunday Mass; in a sense, they are *Eucharistic* visions. We are celebrating this All Saints in what the Holy Father has named the Year of the Eucharist, running from now to next October. And perhaps it can help us to brighten our vision of the saints to know it is a Eucharistic vision.

In union with the whole Church, prays the priest in the heart of the Mass, we honour Mary, the ever-virgin mother of Jesus Christ our Lord and God; Joseph her husband, the apostles and martyrs, Peter and Paul, and *all the saints* ... For ourselves too, we ask some share in the fellowship of your apostles and martyrs, with John the Baptist, Stephen, Matthias and *all the saints*. (Eucharistic Prayer I)

Every Mass is Calvary, every Mass is the Resurrection, every Mass is Pentecost, and every Mass is a feast of all saints. The saints are before the Throne and are seeing, eyes enlightened, the slain but risen Lamb, returned in glory to the bosom of his Father. And at the altar we are with them, seeing the same in sacramental form: the body and blood of the Lamb offered to the Father in the Spirit. We are on one side, so to speak, of the altar, the visible side; they are on the other, invisible but real. Like John we see the saints in the Eucharist – and the Eucharist in the saints: 'they have washed their robes white again in the blood of the Lamb' (7.14); they are the glorified body of Christ; the *res* of the sacrament. If we want to understand what the Eucharist is, we can look at the saints. 'I, John, saw.' The saints ate the Thanksgiving and now they are nothing but gratitude. They ate the Sacrifice and have become a sacrifice of praise. They ate the one Bread and they make one Body. They ate the Love and drank the Life and they live that Love to the full. They are the Eucharist completed. They ate and drank the very Person who is poor in spirit, gentle, mourning, merciful, pure and peaceful, and became what they ate. They partook of the Holy Thing and have become holy ones. There is a feast of All Saints because there is the Eucharist, and each of us can say, 'It will be thanks to the Eucharist, that I, too, become a saint.'

Note
1. This quotation is taken from the Jerusalem Bible.

22

The Parousia: Sure and Certain Hope

From the fig tree learn its lesson: as soon as its branch becomes tender and puts forth its leaves, you know that summer is near. So also, when you see all these things, you know that he is near, at the very gates.

(Mt 24.32–33)

A strange text, perhaps, for a winter's night, but allowable, I hope, for Advent eve.

Our Lord will come again. This is part of our faith. The New Testament is full of it. 'This Jesus,' say the angels of the Ascension, 'who was taken up from you into heaven, will come in the same way as you saw him go into heaven' (Acts 1.11). 'For the Lord himself will descend from heaven,' St Paul elaborates, 'with a cry of command, with the archangel's call, and with the sound of the trumpet of God' (1 Thess 4.16). 'And then they will see the Son of Man,' says the Lord through St Luke, 'coming in a cloud with power and great glory' (Lk 21.27). 'Behold he is coming with the clouds,' confirms Revelation, 'and every one will see him, every one who pierced him' (Rev 1:7). So 'now, little children,' adds St John, 'abide in him, so that when he appears we may have confidence and not shrink from him in shame at his coming' (1 Jn 2.28).

Doubtless each of the New Testament writers and writings has his and its own perspectives, and pages upon pages are written on Pauline, Johannine, Synoptic eschatologies (in the plural). If one wants to get confused, one can. But even the

Anchor Bible Dictionary, hardly servile to doctrinal tradition, rises to this:

> The belief in the Parousia ... is firmly rooted in all strands of the New Testament, though the expectation can be referred to apart from the word or by use of other terms. Even in those books where the person of Christ does not loom large (like the letter of James), the Parousia of the Lord ... is referred to (Jas 5.7).[1]

'Come, Lord Jesus' is a prayer that springs from the heart of the New Testament.

The Greek word *parousia* – much used nowadays – denotes the arrival or presence of someone, their advent. In Christian language it principally denotes the coming of Christ in glory at the end, his Second Coming or Return. Synonyms are 'revelation', 'epiphany' and, from the Latin, 'advent'.

The Apostles' Creed sums up the New Testament witness and the faith of the Church: 'He will come again to judge the living and dead.' The Nicene Creed is slightly more elaborate: 'He will come again in glory to judge the living and the dead, and his kingdom will have no end.' 'We proclaim your death and we confess your resurrection, until you come', we sing after the Consecration at Mass, or as the English powerfully has it: 'Christ has died, Christ is risen, Christ will come again.' Scripture, the Creeds, the Liturgy: they all say the same.

'Devotion falls back upon dogma,' said Newman, and so we may wonder, what does this imply for our outlook and life? What can the Parousia, this future certainty, do for our faith, hope and love? To be honest, I don't have anything insightful or sparkling to say, but let me venture something.

One obvious path for a conference on the Parousia would be the in-your-face one: 'And when did *you* last think of the Parousia, you walking specimen of eschatological amnesia? Isn't it about time you started?' – put less crudely, no doubt! But there is a gentler way. The Parousia is a mystery of the Lord, like his incarnation, birth, epiphany and so on. The fact

that this is a mystery which has not yet 'happened' no more
relegates it to irrelevance than does the fact of the other
mysteries having already 'happened' condemn them to obliv-
ion. As their effectiveness continues, so it is already at work.
They are alive through memory; the Parousia is alive through
hope. And so perhaps the grace we need is i) to recognize this
presence of the Parousia in us and among us, its signs, and ii)
to follow them up, endorse them, cultivate them.

> Look at the fig tree and all the trees; as soon as they come out in
> leaf, you can see for yourselves and know that summer is already
> near. So also, when you see these things taking place, you know
> that the kingdom of God is near. (Lk 21.30–31)

This leads on. The Parousia, and all it entails, is one of
Christianity's central affirmations. It can't be taken away with
impunity. In this sense, it is comparable to and, of course, all
bound up with the Incarnation of the Lord, his saving death
on the Cross and his glorious Resurrection. Together they
form four great pillars of the house of faith. And just as in
some sense, the whole of Christianity is concentrated in the
Incarnation – 'God became man so that man might become
God', say that and there's nothing more to say – and is all
found again in the Cross – the epiphany of God's 'love to the
end' – and in the Resurrection – that love raising the world;
so it is all gathered up too in the Parousia, in the expectation
of God's final victory over evil, the resurrection of the body
and the inauguration of a new heaven and a new earth. So just
as Christianity, from one point of view, is wholly faith, and
from another wholly love, so again – in the light of the Parousia – it is wholly *hope*. That is why St Peter can say: 'Always
be ready to make your defence to anyone who demands from
you an accounting of the *hope* that is in you' (1 Pet 3:15).
That is what the Christian carries within him: hope. It's why
St Paul can say, 'We know that the whole creation has been
groaning in labour pains until now; and not only the creation
but we ourselves, who have the first fruits of the Spirit, groan
inwardly while we wait for adoption, the redemption of our
bodies. For in *hope* we were saved' (Rom 8.22–24). It's why

in the Letter to the Hebrews, faith is famously defined as 'the substance [or assurance] of things hoped for' (Heb 11.1). 'For here we have no lasting city, but we are looking for the city that is to come' (Heb 13.14). In the light of the Parousia and all it will bring with it, the Church and the Christian receive a special kind of inner profile, a shape, a distinctive face, a face turned to this future, 'as we wait in joyful hope for the coming of our Saviour Jesus Christ'. And this can take over everything.

Yes, the Parousia is alive and active in us when we *hope*. 'But if we hope for what we do not see, we wait for it with patience.' The present time – between Pentecost and the Parousia – is, says the *Catechism*, 'a time of waiting and watching' (672). What is the monastic life? One of my novice master's answers was 'patience and prayer'. That is hope in practice. Prayer is waiting and watching – keeping vigil, and patience covers the rest. St Francis de Sales used to say, *Voir sans regarder*, 'see without looking'. We see a lot of things in life, but many of them it's better not to look at. 'Turn away my eyes that they may not behold vanity' (Ps 118:37). Balancing that, I once saw prayer described as *Regarder sans voir*. It's looking, looking out, but not yet seeing. Prayer and patience, patience and prayer. Why, in apparent contradiction to several statements of the Gospel, is the Coming delayed? The reason is not on Christ's side. Since his Ascension – says the *Catechism* – it 'has been imminent', 'could be accomplished at any moment' (673). It is delayed for us, for the sake of the fig tree: another round of manure, another year to sprout.

> And the days of our life are lengthened and a respite allowed us for this very reason, that we may amend our ways, as the Apostle says, 'Do you not realize that God's patience is meant to lead you to repentance?' (*Rule*, Prologue 36–37; Rom 2.4)

We all have a beginning, a middle and an end. In the beginning we are called to learn – all always are – but the young embody it. In the middle we are called to good works – all always are – but those in middle life embody it. Those approaching their end are called to wait in patience for the Lord to save, and so doing they show us all the inmost heart of the monastic, the Christian life. Take away the Parousia, take away eternal life, and what dignity do the elderly have? Are they anything more than 'crumblies'? Anything more than a problem when there's no horizon other than this life? Allow the Parousia in, and perspectives can change. Even when they no longer seem to pray, they are prayer. 'Patience and prayer'. Sometimes there's talk of the 'eschatological nature' of the monastic life. What that means is, 'Let them bear with the greatest patience one another's infirmities, whether of body or character' (*Rule* 72:5). And patience could be defined as 'moving together', even 'moving at the pace of the slowest'.

If the Parousia is in us, if the Lord's coming is coming closer, when we hope and pray and endure (together), it is also among us in another, sacramental way: in the Eucharist. It was Fr Paul McPartlan who opened my eyes to this, and I have found the same in something of Joseph Ratzinger. In the Eucharist, the Parousia is really anticipated. And the true interpretation of those New Testament passages which paint the Lord's coming in vivid colours: the trumpet blast, the collapse of the elements, the coming on the clouds, the angelic escort, the rising up of the elect to greet the Lord in the air etc.: the true interpretation is Eucharistic. The imagery is liturgical imagery with roots in the Jewish liturgy and in the liturgy that surrounded ancient Rulers. 'But in those days, after that tribulation, the sun will be darkened, and the moon will not give its light, and the stars will be falling from heaven, and the powers in the heavens will be shaken. And then they will see the Son of Man coming in clouds with great power and glory. And then he will send out the angels, and gather his elect from the four winds, from the ends of the earth to the ends of heaven.' That is the Parousia according to St Mark (13.24–27). It is also the Mass. I don't need to elaborate that, surely. Every element in that description is fulfilled at every Eucharist. The Mass is the Parousia, the world-transforming Presence, under wraps, so to speak, hidden, the mystery of *faith*. And the Parousia will be the liturgy, the Eucharist, unveiled, revealed as the Truth and the Life at the heart of the world, the Medicine of Immortality. 'From the fig tree learn its lesson: as soon as its branch becomes tender and puts forth its leaves, you know that summer is near. So also, when you see these things taking place, you know that he is near, at the very gates' (Mk 13.28). One of Newman's Advent sermons is called, 'Worship, the Preparation for Christ's Coming.'

At the end of 2 Timothy, Paul, an old man now, is giving a final charge to his beloved disciple and then reflects back, one last time, on himself: 'I have fought the good fight, I have finished the race, I have kept the faith. From now on there is reserved for me the crown of righteousness, which the Lord, the righteous judge, will give me on that day, and not only to me, but also to all who have loved his appearing' (2 Tim 4.7–8). It is a remarkable phrase. It's a remarkable definition of Christians, 'at once magnificent, dense and traditional', says Ceslas Spicq. The 'appearing' is certainly the Parousia, the coming in glory at the end, and 'love' here means setting one's love upon, a persevering love of predilection, a faithful attachment, and a longing, a desiring. Elsewhere in the New Testament there is talk of expecting Christ's coming, even of hastening it. Here it is a question of loving it. I haven't spoken about fear. So far as we are not fully Christians, so far as the fig tree is barren, has still not put out all its branches, there is place for fear: fear of the judgment the Parousia brings. Another of Newman's sermons is called precisely, 'Shrinking from Christ's Coming'. It can be a salutary fear. The relationship of fear to love, Judgment to Parousia, is the same as the relationship of the sacrament of Penance to that of the Eucharist. But joyful hope, the Table of the Lord and perfect love are surely meant to have the last word in us.

Let me end with three quotations. First, St Augustine quotes St Paul:

'I want you to be free from preoccupation'. One who is free from preoccupation looks forward with confidence to the coming of his Lord; for what kind of love for Christ would it be, to be afraid of his Coming? Are we not ashamed of such an attitude, brothers and sisters? We love him, and yet dread his coming? Are we sure, in that case, that we do love him? Do we perhaps not love our sins more? Let us rather hate the sins, and love him who will come to punish sins ... These are the oblations most pleasing to God: mercy, humility, confession, peace, charity. Let us bring him these, and then we can await without anxiety the coming of the judge who 'will judge the world with equity, the peoples in his truth'.[2]

St John Chrysostom:

How, it may be asked, is one to 'love the appearing' of Christ? By rejoicing at his coming; and he who rejoices at his coming will perform works worthy of his joy; he will throw away his substance if need be, and even his life, to obtain future blessings, to be thought worthy to behold that second coming in a fitting state, in confidence, in brightness and glory. This is to 'love his appearing'. He who loves his coming will do everything to ensure, before his general coming, a particular coming to himself. And how, you will say, is this possible? Listen to Christ who says, 'If a man love me he will keep my words, and my Father and I will come to him, and make our dwelling with him'. And think how great a privilege it is that he who will appear to all generally should promise to come to us in particular: for he says, he 'will come and make our dwelling with him'. If anyone 'loves his appearing', he will do everything to invite him to himself, and to hold on to him, so that the light may shine upon him. Let there be nothing unworthy of his coming, and he will soon take up his dwelling with us.[3]

Finally, Newman, a vision in winter, from a sermon, *The Greatness and Littleness of Human Life*:

Heaven at present is out of sight, but in due time, as snow melts and discovers what it lay upon, so will this visible creation fade away before those greater splendours which are behind it, and on which at present it depends. In that day shadows will retire, and the substance. The sun will grow pale and be lost in the sky, but it will be before the radiance of him whom it does but image, the Sun of righteousness, with healing on his wings, who will come forth in visible form, as a bridegroom out of his chamber, while his perishable type decays. The stars that surround it will be replaced by saints and angels circling his throne. Above and below, the clouds of the air, the trees of the field, the waters of the great deep will be found impregnated with the forms of ever-lasting spirits, the servants of God which do his pleasure. And our own mortal bodies will then be found in like manner to contain within them an inner man, which will then receive its due proportions, as the soul's harmonious organ, instead of that gross mass of flesh and blood which sight and touch are sensible of. For this glorious manifestation the whole creation is at present in travail, earnestly desiring that it may be accomplished in its season. These are thoughts to make us eagerly and devoutly say, 'Come, Lord Jesus, to end the time of waiting, of darkness, of turbulence, of disputing, of sorrow, of care.'[4]

Notes

1. *Anchor Bible Dictionary* (Doubleday, New York, 1992), art. '*Parousia*', V, p. 166.
2. St Augustine, *Exposition of Psalm 95*, 14, 15.
3. St John Chrysostom, *Commentary on II Tim*, 4.8.
4. Newman, *Parochial and Plain Sermons*, 4, 14, pp. 223–4.

23

Christian Joy

I received recently a copy of the first letter Fr Maurus wrote to Frank Duff after becoming a monk. Its date is 10 May 1953, ie, after his final profession and ordination. In it he says this:

> About a year after profession, happiness began to flow in the inner streams in a fashion that was entirely new to my experience. I was quite distressed and uncomfortable at it for a while. Then I found the Nazi slogan was true. 'Strength through Joy', they used to chant. I surrendered to the Spirit of Joy as far as I could. I put the qualification because even here, with the gift coming unsolicited, it remains true that the inevitable is attained and preserved only with great effort. The joy of the Spirit has no roots in the natural. The surrender lies precisely in the surrendering of natural action to achieve this end, abandoning to the 'providing' of circumstance. The qualification of 'as far as I could' refers to a feeling that I could use the gift more than I do. I might, as it were, give it away more generously![1]

It is a pattern – *not* everybody's, but still not uncommon – that joy comes into one's life *after* choosing the difficult good of God's will, and once the surrender of the natural desires has reached a certain depth. The joy comes in as a confirmation. Then, Fr Maurus himself: he prided himself on looking 'lugubrious' and regularly inveighed against the pursuit of 'happiness'. One learned to avoid the word when talking to him! But he was a joyful man. That was shown me once sitting in the library in the dark. In came Fr Maurus thinking there was no one there. He walked up and down the library singing antiphons and snatches of hymns to Our Lady, all of them joyful. And there was his comment on the famous Introit of the Third Sunday of Advent, 'Rejoice in the Lord always': 'When the Liturgy tells you to rejoice, you do!'

So, JOY. A second quotation from the Russian theologian in exile, Alexander Schmemann:

> And yet, from its very beginning Christianity has been the procla- mation of joy, of the only possible joy on earth. It rendered impossible all joy we usually think of as possible. But within this impossibility, at the very bottom of this darkness, it announced and conveyed a new all-embracing joy, and with this joy it trans- formed the End into a Beginning. Without the proclamation of this joy Christianity is incomprehensible. It is only as joy that the Church was victorious in the world and it lost the world when it lost the joy, when it ceased to be the witness of it. Of all accu- sations against Christians, the most terrible one was uttered by Nietzsche when he said that Christians had no joy . . .
>
> 'For, behold, I bring you good tidings of great joy' – thus begins the Gospel, and its end is: 'And they worshipped him and returned to Jerusalem with great joy . . .' (Lk 2.10; 24.52) And we must recover the meaning of this great joy. We must if possi- ble partake of it, before we discuss anything else – programmes and missions, projects and techniques.
>
> Joy, however, is not something one can define or analyze. One enters into joy. 'Enter thou into the joy of thy Lord' (Mt 25.21). And we have no other means of entering into that joy, no way of understanding it, except through the one action which from the beginning has been for the Church both the source and the fulfil- ment of joy, the very sacrament of joy, the Eucharist.[2]

We must be ever evangelizing ourselves, and part of that is saying to oneself, often, resonantly, loudly: Christianity *is* joy! If it is the Kingdom of God, if it is the forgiveness of sins, justification, adoption as sons, if it is grace and peace and redemption, if it is resurrection and life, if it is God's last word to mankind, if it is the coming of Christ and the outpour- ing of the Spirit, then it is joy. It cannot be anything else. 'For the kingdom of God,' said St Paul to the Romans, 'does not mean food and drink but righteousness and peace and joy in the Holy Spirit' (Rom 14.17). There is a real link between the New Testament's chosen word for grace, *charis*, and its chosen word for joy, *chara*. So, as Schmemann points out, the Gospel of grace – specifically the Gospel of St. Luke – begins and ends with 'great joy'. Indeed, it moves from the proclamation of the great joy by the angels of Bethlehem to the assimilation of it by the disciples. And that is the path for us.

Christianity is joy. Said Ceslas Spicq, the Dominican philologist:

> The distinguishing characteristic of the Judeo-Christian religion is joy [*chara*] ... [This] contrasts with the pessimism and despair of first-century paganism. This explains why a large proportion of the occurrences of *chara* in the papyri are of Christian origin, why pagan occurrences of the word are so rare, and especially why pagan joy is never that of the soul ... hence there is no religious parallel to the New Testament.[3]

In the sculpture of the first century, the eyes often express sorrow, 'a sort of hopeless stupor'. Hence, as Schmemann says, it was as joy that the Church was victorious in the world, 'and it lost the world when it lost the joy'.

Christianity is joy, ineradicably, and Benedict XVI has said so already, more than once. And if it is, this means that joy really exists, is not an illusion, is objective, and it really exists for us, for me. It is there waiting. It means – to quote biblical scholars – 'in disagreement with the prevailing modern understanding, [that] joy primarily refers not to an involuntary and internal "emotion"',[4] but 'has its source beyond mere earthly, human joy. It is joy in the Lord, and therefore outside ourselves. This is why Paul constantly reminds his readers of its existence and exhorts them to manifest it.'[5] 'Finally, my brethren, rejoice in the Lord' (Phil 3.1); 'Rejoice in the Lord always; again I will say, Rejoice' (Phil 4.4); 'Rejoice in your hope' (Rom 12.12) Even in the natural realm, of course, joy has this originally external character: there is an objective something or someone which gives me joy. Now, beyond all such, beyond all wholesome, never-to-be-despised natural joys, beyond green and flowing things, beyond friendship and human love and the birth of children, beyond food and drink, good health and happiness in work, music and dancing and coming home and victory and every form of beauty; beyond all these things so often acclaimed in the Bible, there is a new, unquenchable joy, free from the tyranny of mortality, the joy of the crucified and risen Christ, paschal joy. Wherever there is life, there is joy. Where there is life stronger than sin and death, there will be the 'great joy'. And into this joy we are baptized and confirmed, and into this, in the measure of our faith, hope and love, especially our love, we enter more and more, until it overtakes us like a flood as joy everlasting.

If the Eucharist is a daily entry into joy, the annual sacrament, in the mind of the Church, is Easter. And it is often the Easterners who have been the most eloquent here. Take this from another Russian emigré, Sergius Bulgakov:

> On Easter night when the Paschal procession going round the Church comes to the closed doors and stops, our souls are touched by an almost imperceptible and yet spiritually significant instant of uncomprehending, questioning silence: 'Who will roll away the stone for us from the door of the tomb?' And will the tomb be empty, with Christ risen? When the doors are opened, before the Sign of the Cross, and during the singing of the exultant Paschal hymn, we enter the Church all gleaming with lights, and our hearts are flooded with joy, for Christ is risen from the dead. And then the Paschal miracle is performed in our souls. For we 'see the Resurrection of Christ'. 'Having purified our senses', we see 'Christ shining', and 'as He comes out of the tomb we go to meet Christ, the Bridegroom'. Then we forget where we are, we pass out of ourselves, time stops, and we enter 'the Sabbath rest of the People of God'. In the radiance of the white light of Easter, earthly colours are dimmed, and the soul sees only 'the unapproachable light of the Resurrection'; 'now all things are filled with light, heaven and earth and the underworld'. On Easter night it is given to man to experience in advance the life of the age to come, to enter into the Kingdom of Glory, the Kingdom of God. The language of our world has no words to express the

revelation of Easter night, for it is a mystery of the age to come, which has a 'silent language' of its own. The perfect joy given to us on this night, according to the Lord's promise, is indeed the Holy Spirit, who by the Father's will reveals to us the risen Christ. The Holy Spirit is the joy which exists within the Holy Trinity, the Father's joy in the Son and the Son's in the Father; He is also the joy that is within us because of the Resurrection of Christ. Through him we see the risen Christ; He is, within us, the light of Christ's Resurrection.[6]

Let the New Testament be our guide. 'Enter into the joy of your Lord.' First of all, there is the joy of Christ himself. He spreads it even before his birth. 'Rejoice, full of grace,' says the angel to Mary. 'For behold, when the voice of your greeting came to my ears, the babe in my womb leaped for joy,' (Lk 1.44) says Elizabeth, and Mary can only respond, 'My soul magnifies the Lord and my spirit rejoices in God my Saviour.' Christ's birth is a benign hurricane of joy, taking up angels and men, Zechariah and Elizabeth, Mary and Joseph, the shepherds and the wise men. This is indeed a very Lucan theme, but not only so. The very same 'great joy' the angel proclaims to the shepherds possesses St Matthew's wise men on seeing the star. Then, with the public ministry, this joy spreads wider still. Jesus is the prophet proclaiming the acceptable year of the Lord, the Great Jubilee (Lk 4.19). He is the bridegroom, turning the water of daily life into torrents of wine. 'And Jesus said to them, "Can you make wedding guests fast while the bridegroom is with them?"' (Lk 5.33) So, 'all the people rejoiced at all the glorious things that were done by him' (Lk 13.17); there was joy in heaven over the finding of lost sheep and coins and sons (Lk 15); 'The seventy returned with joy, saying, "Lord, even the demons are subject to us in your name"' (Lk 9.17); '[Zacchaeus] made haste and came down and received him joyfully' (Lk 19.6); even Abraham had seen this day and rejoiced (Jn 8.56). 'Go and tell John what you have seen and heard: the blind receive their sight, the lame walk, lepers are cleansed, and the deaf hear, the dead are raised up, the poor have good news preached to them. And blessed is he who takes no offence at me' (Lk 7.22–23).

But no one gives what he does not have. Jesus *has* joy, in a special way, from the moment of his baptism, when he is anointed with the oil of gladness, the Holy Spirit himself. When the Gospel is received by the poor, 'in that same hour he rejoiced in the Holy Spirit and said, "I thank you, Father, Lord of heaven and earth"' (Lk 10.21). And in the Johannine Last Discourse, it is not only his peace he promises his disciples but his joy. 'These things I have spoken to you, that my joy may be in you, and that your joy may be full' (Jn 15.11). 'So you have sorrow now, but I will see you again and your hearts will rejoice, and no one will take your joy from you' (Jn 16.22). That is because it is *his* joy. If Luke and Matthew proclaim 'great joy', for John it is 'fullness of joy'. This is language being stretched to receive something hitherto unknown. 'But now I am coming to thee,' prays Jesus in the priestly prayer, 'and these things I speak in the world, that they may have my joy fulfilled in themselves' (Jn 17.13). So for 'the joy that was set before him [he] endured the cross, despising the shame, and is seated at the right hand of the throne of God' (Heb 12.2), in joy, giving what he has. 'So they [the women] departed quickly from the tomb with fear and great joy, and ran to tell his disciples. And behold, Jesus met them and said, *"Chairete!* Rejoice!"' (Mt 28.9). 'And while they still disbelieved for joy, and wondered, he said to them, "Have you anything here to eat?"' (Lk 24.41).

'Enter into the joy of your Lord.' Christianity is joy. It's a Trinitarian conspiracy. The Father by raising his crucified Son has thrown open the doors of joy. And we enter them in the light of the Spirit. 'Through Him we see the risen Christ.' 'Everything we can say that is good and joyful and sweet, all of that is the Holy Spirit',[7] says St Aelred. Christian joy is a fruit of the Spirit, says St Paul, the first after love (Gal 5.22). It is 'joy in the Holy Spirit' (Rom 14.17), 'joy inspired by the Holy Spirit' (1 Thess 1.6). The disciples, says St Luke in *Acts*, 'were filled with joy and with the Holy Spirit' (Acts 13.52). And the Spirit takes us into joy, first of all, by opposing the flesh and its cravings, putting to death the deeds of the lower nature, triumphing over the sin and sadness which dwell within us, our proclivity to false joys, our genius for clinging to the very things that make us miserable. The entry into joy, from our side, is by renunciation of our own will, by not loving our own will nor delighting in fulfilling our own desires, by making ourselves, if you like, an empty tomb from which the hidden, waiting Joy can erupt. As fallen beings we are sad, *ipso facto*. And for each of us, Life has impinged on a certain temperament, has hurt us, and we have added to the hurt by sinning. And so we are sad. We are sad because we do not have what we want or do have what we do not want. But as redeemed we are joyful, *ipso facto*. And the more the Holy Spirit pours the love of God into our hearts, through faith, through prayer, through the sacraments, the more the inner streams will run with joy, whatever our temperament, whatever our past. This is the Holy Spirit at work, and the saints, from Mary and John the Baptist onwards, are our companions in this joy. They know the secret: St Francis, St Philip Neri, St Seraphim of Sarov whose greeting always was: 'Christ is risen, my joy!' Every evening at Vespers, we can echo Mary's joy, she whom the Litany calls the 'Cause of our Joy'.

There seems to be a moment in people's lives when they do, in a new way, enter into joy, are 'surprised by joy'. There are breakthroughs into joy. They are always breakthroughs into inner freedom, not into getting things but into letting go. I once read of the Canadian Jesuit philosopher, Bernard Lonergan, that at about forty he entered into joy and was in it for the rest of his life. Remember our Br John Ogilvie at the end; after much suffering and frustration he too entered into joy.

What else to say? Seven thoughts.

Christian joy is very much bound up with prayer. If a Christian is unfaithful to prayer, he will enter into sadness, as sure as night follows day. If he is faithful to prayer, he will, at some level, be joyful, come what may. And the liturgy – sung praise – is our witness to Joy, our answer to Nietzsche.

Christian joy is what one might call an internal-external. It is outside us within us, and if we find the way to our hearts we will find the way to joy. It is there, like Christ in the tomb, waiting to rise.

The 'happy-clappy' error (and there are many worse) is to

think that we can always emotionally enjoy joy; that it can always be at the wheel of our emotional life. But it can't be. On the other side, though, it is true that there is nothing the Christian must so avoid as despondency. He must fight every attempt of sadness (and of anger) to take the wheel. 'Let no one be saddened or disturbed in the house of God' (*Rule* 31.19). I may not be directly responsible for what I feel, but I am responsible for what I do with what I feel.

Christian joy – the Apostles discovered, and it must have been a shock – is joy in affliction. It proved that what Christ had said was actually true: 'Blessed are you when men revile you and persecute you and utter all kinds of evil against you falsely on my account. Rejoice and be glad, for your reward is great in heaven' (Mt 5.11–12). 'Then they left the presence of the council, rejoicing that they were counted worthy to suffer dishonour for the name' (Acts 5.41). 'In this you rejoice [the hope of salvation], even if now for a little while you have had to suffer various trials' (1 Pet 1:6). 'Rejoice so far as you share Christ's sufferings, that you may also rejoice and be glad when his glory is revealed' (1 Pet 4.13). 'Count it all joy, my brethren, when you meet with various trials' (Jas 1:2). 'You joyfully accepted the plundering of your property,' says the writer to the Hebrews (10.34), 'since you knew that you yourselves had a better possession and an abiding one.' 'You received the word in much affliction,' says St Paul to the Thessalonians, 'with joy inspired by the Holy Spirit' (1 Thess 1:6). This unexpected marriage of affliction and joy becomes one of Paul's leitmotifs, especially in his dealings with the difficult Corinthians: 'I have great confidence in you; I have great pride in you; I am filled with comfort. With all our affliction, I am overjoyed (more stretching of language: "I *super-abound* with joy")' (2 Cor 7.4). It crops up again writing to the Philippians from gaol: imprisonment is an affliction, but Paul sees the good flowing from it, 'and in that I rejoice' (Phil 1.18). Hence the famous line in Colossians: 'Now I rejoice in my sufferings for your sake, and in my flesh I complete what is lacking in Christ's afflictions for the sake of his body, the Church' (Col 1.24). St Benedict echoes all this when he has joy on the fourth step of humility.

Christian joy is also joy at the success of the Church's mission, at the spreading of the faith, the conversion of sinners. Christian joy finally is a joy in waiting for its full unleashing in heaven. It is joy in hope, the joy of spiritual desire. 'Although you have not seen him, you love him; and even though you do not see him now, you believe in him and rejoice with an indescribable and glorious joy (more straining for words!), for you are receiving the outcome of your faith, the salvation of your souls' (1 Pet 1:8–9).

All I can do, like the angel at Bethlehem, is proclaim that Joy exists. Then we have to want it, or want more of it. And why not? The more the better. And the Psalms have lovely prayers for our hearts to use: 'Give me again the joy of your help' (50.14); 'Give joy to your servant, O Lord, for to you I lift up my soul' (85.4); 'Give us joy to balance our affliction, for the years when we knew misfortune' (89.15; 'This is the day that the Lord has made; let us rejoice and be glad in it!' (117.24).

Notes

1. Fr Maurus Deegan was a monk of Pluscarden Abbey from 1948–2005.
2. Alexander Schmemann, *The World as Sacrament* (Darton, Longman, Todd, London, 1966), pp. 26–27.
3. Ceslas Spicq (ed.), *Theological Lexicon of the New Testament*, vol. III Hendrickson Publishers Inc., Massachusetts, 1994), pp. 498–499.
4. *Exegetical Dictionary of the New Testament*, vol. 3 (Eerdmans, Grand Rapids, Michigan, 1990), p. 454.
5. *The New International Dictionary of New Testament Theology*, vol. 2 (Zondervan, Grand Rapids, Michigan, 1986), p. 359.
6. Sergius Bulgakov, in *Ultimate Questions*, (ed.) A. Schmemann (St Vladimir's Seminary Press, New York, 1977), pp. 299–300.
7. St Aelred of Rievaulx, *Mirror of Charity*, I, 20, 57.

Printed in the United Kingdom
by Lightning Source UK Ltd.
118739UK00001B/184-471